Catholic Bible Study

Romans
and
Ephesians

by

Most Reverend Michael J. Byrnes, S.T.D.

and

Laurie Watson Manhardt, Ph.D.

Emmaus Road Publishing
1468 Parkview Circle, Steubenville, OH 43952
740-264-9535

All rights reserved. Published in 2019
Printed in the United States of America

Library of Congress Control Number: 2019940611
ISBN 978-1-949013-88-7

Cover design and layout by
Jacinta Calcut, Image Graphics & Design, www.image–gd.com

Cover artwork:
Saint Paul Writing His Epistles, by Valentin de Boulogne
and Holy Spirit, by Melissa Dayton

Nihil obstat: Very Reverend Albert A. Della Russo, JCL, *Censor Deputatis*

Imprimi potest
+Most Reverend Gerald M. Barbarito, DD, JCL
Bishop of Palm Beach
Feast of Saints Philip and James the Less
May 3, 2019

The *Nihil obstat* and *Imprimi potest* are ecclesiastical declarations that a book or
pamphlet is free of doctrinal or moral error. No implication is contained therein that those
who have attested to this agree with the contents, opinions, or statements expressed.

For additional information on the "Come and See ~ Catholic Bible Study"
series visit www.CatholicBibleStudy.net

Catholic Bible Study

Romans and Ephesians

Introduction

We know that in everything,
God works for good with those who love him,
who are called according to his purpose. . . .
For I am sure that neither death, nor life, nor angels, nor principalities,
nor things present, nor things to come, nor powers, nor height, nor depth,
nor anything else in all creation,
will be able to separate us from the love of God in Christ Jesus our Lord.
Romans 8:30, 38–39

The Letter of Paul to the Romans shines as a jewel among the Pauline epistles, appearing first in the Bible after Acts, even though other letters were written earlier. It deserves to be read in its entirety, before pulling verses out of context. The sixteen chapters can be read in about an hour. In Romans, Paul provides a clear picture of the Good News of salvation in Jesus Christ for all people, Jews and Gentiles alike.

Of all of the human authors of the Bible, Saint Paul has written more books than any other writer. Thirteen of the twenty-seven books of the New Testament are attributed to Pauline authorship. For about the first thousand years of Christianity, the Letter to the Hebrews was also attributed to Paul, but that authorship has since been questioned. Since the writing style of Hebrews differs greatly from other Pauline letters, the author of Hebrews remains a mystery at this time.

Even though Paul dictates his own words in the Letter to the Romans to his scribe Tertius to write down (Romans 16:22), Paul clearly claims his authorship at the very beginning of the letter: *Paul, a servant of Jesus Christ, called to be an apostle, set apart for the gospel of God* (Romans 1:1). Since Peter and Paul were both martyred in Rome in AD 64, it is believed that Paul may have written this letter while he was in Corinth, staying with Gaius, around the year AD 57.

God's righteousness radiates in Paul's Letter to the Romans. Beginning with the contrast between the wickedness of sinful humanity and the clear evidence of God's perfect goodness, Paul establishes the need for salvation for pagans, as well as for God's chosen people, who have failed to honor their covenant relationship with God in faithfully obeying the law. Each person must choose between continuing in slavery to sin or believing in Jesus Christ and accepting the grace of justification and the righteousness that comes through faith in Him.

Paul begins by demonstrating everyone's need for a Savior. While affirming the privileged place of the Jewish People and their primacy in election, he reveals Jesus Christ as the Messiah and Redeemer of the world. Then he proceeds to show the practical ways in which sinners may receive God's grace and respond to the leadings of the Holy Spirit. He identifies the characteristics of true Christians and the various gifts given by the Holy Spirit for the building up of the body of Christ. Finally, Paul points his readers to the glory that is yet to be revealed to those who believe.

What You Need

In order to do this Bible Study, you will need a Catholic Bible and the Catechism of the Catholic Church (CCC). The Catechism is available in most bookstores, and it can be easily accessed on the Internet, without charge at these websites: http://www.usccb.org/beliefs-and-teachings/what-we-believe/catechism/catechism-of-the-catholic-church/ or at http://www.vatican.va/archive/ENG0015/_INDEX.HTM

Remember that the Catholic Bible has seventy-three books. If you find Maccabees in your Bible's table of contents, you have a complete Catholic Bible. The Council of Hippo approved these seventy-three books in AD 393, and this has remained the official canon of Sacred Scripture since the fourth century. The Council of Trent in AD 1546 reaffirmed these divinely inspired books as the canon of the Bible.

For Bible study purposes, choose a word-for-word, literal translation rather than a paraphrase of the Bible. An excellent English translation is the Revised Standard Version Catholic Edition (RSVCE) Bible. **Because of different verse numbering in various Bible translations, the RSVCE second edition by Ignatius Press will be the easiest to consult to complete the home study questions in the *Come and See ~ Catholic Bible Study* series.**

How To Do This Bible Study

1. Pray to the Holy Spirit to enlighten your mind and spirit.
2. Read the Bible passages for the first chapter.
3. Read the commentary in this book.
4. Use your Bible and Catechism to write answers to the home study questions. Put your answers in your own words in a short phrase or sentence.
5. Watch the videotape lecture that goes with this study.
6. In a small group, share your answers aloud on those questions.
7. End with a short prayer.

Practical Considerations

➤ Ask God for wisdom about whom to study with, where, and when to meet.
➤ Gather a small prayer group to pray for your Bible study, your specific needs, your members, and those you might reach out to invite.
➤ Show this book to your pastor and obtain his approval and direction.
➤ Find an appropriate location. Start in someone's home or in the parish hall if the space is available and the pastor will allow it.
➤ Hire a babysitter for mothers with young children and share the cost amongst everyone, recruit some volunteers to provide childcare, or form a co-op to care for and teach children.

Pray that God will anoint specific people to lead your study. Faithful, practicing Catholics are needed to fill the following positions:

➢ **Teachers**—Pray, read commentaries, and prepare a short wrap-up lecture.
➢ **Prayer Leaders**—Open Bible study with a short prayer.
➢ **Children's Teachers**—Teach the young children who come to Bible study.
➢ **Coordinators**—Communicate with parish personnel about needs for rooms, microphones, and video equipment. Make sure rooms are left in good shape.
➢ **Small Group Facilitators** will be needed for each small group. Try to enlist two mature Catholics who are good listeners to serve together as co-leaders to:

   ❖ Make a nametag and pray for each member of the small group.
   ❖ Meet before the study to pray with other leaders.
   ❖ Discuss all the questions in the lesson each week. Begin and end on time.
   ❖ Make sure that each person in the group shares each week.
   ❖ Make sure that no one person dominates the discussion, including you!
   ❖ Keep the discussion positive and focused on the week's lesson.
   ❖ Speak kindly and charitably. Avoid any negative or uncharitable speech.
   ❖ Listen well! Keep your ears open and your eyes on the person speaking.
   ❖ Give your full attention to the person speaking. Be comfortable with silence.
   ❖ If questions, misunderstandings, or disagreements arise, refer them to the question box for a teacher to research or the parish priest to answer later.
   ❖ Arrange for a social activity each month.

More Practical Considerations

➢ Twelve to fifteen people make the best size for small groups. When you get too many people in a group, break into two smaller groups.
➢ Sit next to the most talkative person in the group and across from the quietest. Use eye contact to encourage quieter people to speak up. Serve and hear from everyone in the group.
➢ Listening in Bible study is just as important as talking. Evaluate each week. Did everyone share? Am I a good listener? Did I really hear what others shared? Was I attentive or distracted? Did I affirm others? Did I talk too much?
➢ Share the overall goal aloud with all of the members of the group. Try to have each person in the group share aloud each time the group meets.
➢ Make sure that people share answers only for those questions on which they have written answers. Don't just share off the top of your head. Really study.
➢ Listen to God as you read His Word. What words or phrases jump out at you and grab your attention? What is God trying to say to you? How can you apply God's Word to your everyday life?

Invite and Welcome Priests and Religious

Ask for the blessing of your pastor before you begin this study. Invite priests, deacons, and religious to come and pray with Bible study members, periodically answer questions from the question box, or give a wrap-up lecture. Accept whatever they can offer to the Bible study group. However, don't expect or demand anything from them. Appreciate that they are very busy and do not add additional burdens to their schedule. Accept with gratitude whatever is offered.

Wrap-Up Lecture

Additional information is available for this study in videotaped lectures, which can be obtained from Emmaus Road Publishing, a part of the Saint Paul Center, in Steubenville, Ohio, 43952. You can obtain DVDs of these lectures by going to www.emmausroad.org or by calling 1-740-264-9535. Videotaped lectures may be used in addition to, or in place of, a wrap-up lecture, depending on your needs.

The word of God is plainly shown in all its strength and wisdom to those who seek out Christ, who is the word, the power and the wisdom of God. This word was with the Father in the beginning, and in its own time was revealed to the apostles, then preached by them and humbly received in faith by believers.

. . . This word then is alive in the heart of the Father, on the lips of the preacher, and in the hearts of those who believe and love him. Since this word is so truly alive, undoubtedly it is full of power.

Saint Baldwin, Bishop of Canterbury (†1190 AD), *Treatise 6: 204, 451.*

A Prayer to the Holy Spirit

O Holy Spirit, Beloved of my soul, I adore You,
enlighten, guide, strengthen, and console me.
Tell me what I ought to say and do, and command me to do it.
I promise to be submissive in everything You will ask of me,
and to accept all that You permit to happen to me,
only show me what is Your will.
Amen.

CHAPTER 1

Gospel Power
Romans 1

I am eager to preach the gospel to you also who are in Rome.
For I am not ashamed of the gospel:
it is the power of God for salvation to everyone who has faith,
to the Jew first and then to the Greek.
For in it the righteousness of God is revealed
through faith for faith;
as it is written:
"He who through faith is righteous shall live."
Romans 1:15–17

The Letter of Paul to the Romans begins with a lengthy salutation from the apostle to the believers in Rome, whom he has never met, but hopes to visit soon. Recall how God called Paul to be an apostle. *But Saul, still breathing threats and murder against the disciples of the Lord, went to the high priest and asked him for letters to the synagogues at Damascus, so that if he found any belonging to the Way, men or women, he might bring them bound to Jerusalem. Now as he journeyed he approached Damascus, and suddenly a light from heaven flashed about him. And he fell to the ground and heard a voice saying to him, "Saul, Saul, why do you persecute me?" And he said, "Who are you, Lord?" And he said, "I am Jesus, whom you are persecuting; but rise and enter the city, and you will be told what you are to do"* (Acts 9:1–6). This amazing story of the conversion of Saul is recounted four times in the New Testament. God transforms Saul—persecutor of the Christians—into Paul, apostle to the Gentiles. Once Paul experiences the transforming love of Christ, he begins to share this good news with zeal.

The righteousness of God—Romans' main theme is the uprightness of God. The absolute perfect holiness of God contrasts with the condition of humanity, estranged from God by sin. Both the Chosen People, who have enjoyed the revelation of God—the privilege of receiving the law and the prophets—and non-Jews, who could experience God by His revelation in creation, have fallen short and sinned against God. This vast chasm between sinful humanity and Almighty God cannot be bridged by anything humans might do. Hence, God intervenes. God's saving justice is manifested as God sends His only begotten Son, Jesus Christ, to redeem humanity. Through the death and Resurrection of Jesus, sinful people can be justified and at peace with God, while waiting for eternal salvation.

The Letter to the Romans is a dense theological letter, offering reflections on the mystery of God and many doctrinal truths, which have been revealed by God. In Romans 1–11, Paul presents the doctrinal portion of the letter. In Romans 12–16, Paul gives a moral exhortation for believers to offer their bodies as a sacrifice of worship to God. The grace received in baptism, and the power of the Holy Spirit, empower believers to turn from sin and live lives pleasing to God. While the prescriptions of the Mosaic Law were good, they lacked the power to enable people to be completely obedient to the law. Believers need the grace of God.

One of the challenges in reading this longest of the Pauline letters presents itself in Paul's use of a simplified style of rhetoric, called diatribe, which was familiar in antiquity. For example, Plato used this style of rhetoric in his arguments with Gorgias. Sometimes Paul speaks as if he has a hidden interlocutor presenting questions or arguments, whom he then addresses. Saint Thomas Aquinas, in writing his *Summa Theologica,* uses a similar format in which he presents a question and then offers several possible responses, before arriving at the truth.

Paul employs Scripture as testimony to prove many of his arguments. At least seventy references to Old Testament Scriptures appear in Paul's Letter to the Romans. One can also easily identify numerous references to the Gospels and other New Testament writings in this lengthy epistle. A well-formed Pauline argument usually ends with the authoritative witness of Sacred Scripture. Readers encounter concentric arguments as well as progressive thought. Sometimes one chapter ends with a thought or a challenge that is resolved later in a subsequent chapter. Opposing arguments may be identified that seem to contradict one another. In reading carefully, one can be able to determine when Paul is using one statement as a foil before presenting the true premise that he intends to advance. Due to these challenges, believers are wise to pray to the Holy Spirit for clarity in understanding when embarking upon this study.

Romans Outline

I. God's Perfect Righteousness versus Humanity's Sinfulness (Romans 1–4)

II. Reconciliation with God through Jesus in the Holy Spirit (Romans 5–11)

III. Christian Moral Living (Romans 12–16)

Greeting—Paul gives a lengthy salutation, identifying himself as a servant, or slave, of Jesus Christ, called to be an apostle, set apart for preaching the gospel of God. He identifies Jesus Christ as the long-awaited son of David, promised by the prophets, the Son of God, proven by His Resurrection from the dead. Jesus is true God and true man. Jesus has always been God, and His Resurrection proves it to people, beyond a doubt. Paul receives the grace of apostleship from Jesus Christ to bring about the obedience of faith among all the nations. Paul's ultimate goal emerges as urging people to have believing trust in Jesus and achieve obedience to God. Like bookends or a framing device, Paul begins and ends this letter with his goal: *to bring about the obedience of faith* (Romans 1:5; 16:26).

> *Through whom we have received grace and apostleship for obedience unto faith . . .* He does not say "for questioning and reasoning," but "for obedience." We were not sent, he says, to argue, but to give what was entrusted into out hands. For when the Master makes some declaration, those who hear are not to bluster about and be meddlesome about what is told them; they have only to accept it. It was for this reason that the apostles were sent: to tell what they had heard, not to add to it anything of their own; and that we, for our part, should believe.
>
> Saint John Chrysostom (AD 344–407),
> *Homilies on the Epistle to the Romans, 1.3*

Paul addresses his letter *to all God's beloved in Rome, who are called to be saints: Grace to you and peace from God our Father and the Lord Jesus Christ* (Romans 1:8). Along with those Romans, reflect on the fact that YOU are also God's beloved. This letter is written for your benefit as well as theirs, and YOU are also called to be a saint. You have been given the grace in baptism to fulfill God's perfect plan for your life, to be obedient to God until the end.

Thanksgiving—Paul, above all, is a man of prayer. He thanks God for the spread of the gospel and the faith of believers around the world. Paul asks God for the opportunity to come to visit the Christian community in Rome. He wants to give a spiritual gift to the Romans to strengthen them, and to receive encouragement and support in return. Paul wants to preach the gospel in Rome. In the first century, Rome was the hub of civilization. Today, some say—if you can make it in New York, you can make it anywhere. In Paul's day, Rome was the center of activity. After writing this letter, Paul would travel to Jerusalem, where he would be arrested and detained as a prisoner. A few years later, Paul would arrive in Rome, an accused prisoner in chains, awaiting trial before Caesar (Acts 21–26).

The power of the gospel—Paul is not ashamed of the gospel, nor should any Christian be embarrassed about the gospel. Each believer must evaluate whether reluctance or embarrassment prevents him or her from sharing the good news with needy souls. Jesus said: *For whoever is ashamed of me and of my words in this adulterous and sinful generation, of him will the Son of man also be ashamed, when he comes in the glory of his Father with the holy angels* (Mark 8:38). Each Christian must understand and embrace the fullness of truth, be able to articulate it, and then have the courage to share this treasure with hungry, lost souls.

What is the power of the gospel? *It is the power of God for salvation to every one who has faith, to the Jew first and also to the Greek. For in it the righteousness of God is revealed through faith for faith; as it is written, "He who through faith is righteous shall live"* (Romans 1:16–17). Faith involves the free gift of God's grace enabling one to believe in God, to repent, and to live in obedience to Him. In order to obtain God's grace, one must understand that he or she is a sinner in need of salvation. God's gift is unmerited and undeserved, but essential.

> What is grace? Something given *gratis*. What is given *gratis*? That which is bestowed rather than paid as owed. If it is owed, it is wages paid, not a gift graciously given. But since you have gotten that grace of faith, you shall be just by faith; for the just man lives by faith. And by living faith you shall deserve well of God; and when you shall have deserved well of God by living by faith, as reward you shall receive immortality and eternal life. And that is grace.
>
> Saint Augustine of Hippo (AD 354–430),
> *Homilies on the Gospel of John, 3.9*

Paul quotes the Prophet Habakkuk: *Behold, he whose soul is not upright in him shall fail, but the righteous shall live by his faith* (Habakkuk 2:4). While destruction and violence surrounded this prophet, he clung to his faith and hope in God. Habakkuk complains to God in the midst of oppression and desolation, and yet he prays and trusts that God will crush the wicked and save those who trust in Him.

God's perfect goodness versus man's sinfulness—Paul defends God's justice. How could a loving God create hell? Why would God punish sinners who never received the law, those who never knew right from wrong? These questions require logic and reason. If unrepentant thieves, rapists, and murderers are not punished or separated from the innocent, the afterlife would be horrific. God's perfect mercy involves God's perfect justice as well. What about those people who never heard the gospel? What about people who live on a desert island and never received the Ten Commandments or heard the Golden Rule? How will God judge them? Are God's ways fair or unfair, just or unjust? The following structure may help.

A — Romans 1:19–21		*For although they knew God they did not honor him*
B — Romans 1:22–24		*God gave them up to the lusts of their hearts to impurity because they exchanged the truth about God for a lie*
B'— Romans 1:25–27		*They exchanged the truth about God for a lie and worshiped and served the creature rather than the Creator*
A'— Romans 1:28–31		*Since they did not see fit to acknowledge God, God gave them up to a base mind and improper conduct*

Human activity warrants divine retribution. Because God has revealed truth, goodness, and beauty in creation, and placed an innate law and reason in human beings' minds, they are without excuse. In the Old Testament, even before God gave the Ten Commandments to Moses forbidding adultery, Jacob's son Joseph knew it would be wrong to accept the sexual advances of Potiphar's wife. Joseph was falsely accused and imprisoned, despite his innocence (Genesis 39:6–20).

Heaven and earth is the sum total of visible things, which seem not only to be ordered to the embellishment of this world but even to the disclosure of invisible things, providing, as it were, an argument for those things which are not seen, as the prophetic utterance announces: *The heavens tell the glory of God, and the firmament proclaims the works of His hands.* The apostle likewise states much the same thing, though in other words, when he says: *His invisible attributes are known through the things which He made.* We easily recognize Him as the Author of the Angels, Dominations, and Powers—He that by the authority of His command made so beautiful a world as this to come into being out of nothing, when before it did not exist, and who gave substance, whether directly or in cause, to those things which before did not exist.

Saint Ambrose of Milan (AD 333–397), *Hexameron 1, 4, 6*

The beauty of creation unfolds before everyone. Sunrise and sunset appears all over the world. The stars in the sky, the waves of the sea, the smell of flowers, the variety of tastes of delicious food, the uniqueness of animals, the softness of a baby's skin, and the epitome of God's creation—man and woman, made in the image and likeness of God—all point to a Creator. Even a young child can ask: who am I, where have I come from, where am I going, why am I here, what is my purpose in life? And a healthy culture provides assistance to the young in providing meaning and purpose for life, forming character, and establishing acceptable boundaries for behavior. Paul asserts that some experiences are universal.

It occurred to Paul that someone might ask him: "Whence do these impious men hold back the truth? Has God ever spoken to any of them? Did they receive the Law, as the nation of Israelites did through Moses? Whence, then do they hold back the truth, even in their very inquiry?" Listen to what follows, and he will show you. *Because what is known of God has been manifested to them: for God has manifested it to them.* Did He manifest it to those to whom He did not give the Law? Hear how He manifested it. *For His invisible attributes are clearly perceived, being understood through the things that have been made.* Ask the world, the beauty of the heavens, the splendor and arrangement of the stars; the sun that suffices for the day; the moon, the comfort of the night; ask the earth, fruitful in herbs and trees, full of animals, adorned with men; ask the sea, filled with so many swimming creatures of every kind; ask the air, replete with so many flying creatures. Ask them all, and see if they do not, as if in a language of their own, answer you: "God made us." Noble philosophers too have sought these things, and have recognized the Artisan by the art.

Saint Augustine of Hippo (AD 354–430), *Sermons 141, 2*

Many who knew God refused to honor Him and gave themselves up to the lusts of their hearts and impurities, exchanging the truth about God for a lie. Therefore, in justice, God gave them up to their base desires and wicked conduct. God gives free will to every human person. Choose truth and life and experience joy. Or choose the lie and spiritual death will follow. Oftentimes, sin is its own punishment.

God has given every good thing for the enjoyment and satisfaction of His children. In the Garden of Eden, everything that God created was good. Adam and Eve were free to enjoy it all, with the exception of one thing. The forbidden fruit became their downfall, and the curse of all humanity.

Righteous living can bring its own reward. People who live ordered, virtuous lives experience peace, love, and joy, even in the midst of challenges and difficulties. Whereas, people who choose evil often fall into a downward spiral that ends in turmoil and destruction. Sin punishes the sinner. The sinner claims to be wise, but becomes a fool. The sinner attempts to rationalize perversity and shameful acts.

In the time of the Prophet Isaiah, a warning came to the people that could be a harbinger for today. *Woe to those who call evil good and good evil* (Isaiah 5:20). People know good and evil, but they now call a mortal sin a civil right. Today there is no excuse. People know God's law, but ignore it or disdain it. This chapter ends with a sober observation. *Though they know God's decree that those who do such things deserve to die, they not only do them but approve those who practice them* (Romans 1:32). Sinners support and encourage one another in their wrongdoing.

The Church does not abandon people who struggle with serious sin. Alcoholics Anonymous and Narcotics Anonymous groups support those who struggle with substance abuse. Overeaters Anonymous helps people who battle the sin of gluttony. Courage groups provide compassionate support for people with same-sex attraction. New groups spring up to help people dealing with addictions to pornography and other sex addiction problems. Whatever temptations people face, the Church strives to help them find the grace and support to live moral lives, which are pleasing to God. May God conform each heart and mind to His Word, and provide the grace needed to live holy lives.

Eve Tushnet, an agnostic raised in a progressive Jewish household, grew up feeling shut out from righteousness. In childhood, Eve displayed a bad temper, selfishness, and general weirdness. In college at Yale, for the first time, Eve a lesbian, met practicing Catholics who talked about their beliefs. She admired them. As she learned about God and the doctrine of the Fall of Man, she discovered an explanation for the sense of wrongness she had felt. What she had been trying to figure out wasn't just about herself and her sexual orientation, but was instead about the human condition. She realized that personal preference was not a good guide to truth and goodness. Eve entered the Catholic Church with minimal faith—Jesus is God, the Savior; this is the Church Jesus founded. Now, Eve writes devotionals and strives to become a saint.

1. Use a dictionary or the Catechism to define "gospel." Romans 1:1–6

2. How can you know that Jesus is the Son of God? Romans 1:4, CCC 648

3. What is faith?

Romans 1:5
Acts 3:16
CCC 26

* Have you ever put your faith in something other than God?

4. In your own words, explain "the obedience of faith."

Romans 1:5
CCC 143
CCC 144

5. To what are you called? Romans 1:6–7

6. Describe Paul's hope and prayer in Romans 1:8–15.

7. In your own words, explain the power of the gospel. Romans 1:16–17

8. What theological virtue is required to believe? CCC 1814

9. Where can one learn about God?

Psalm 19:1–4
Romans 1:18–20
CCC 1147

* How and from whom did you first learn about God?

10. Why did Jesus come and what does wickedness suppress?

John 18:37–38
Romans 1:18

11. What can happen to those who know God but refuse to honor Him?

Romans 1:21	
Romans 1:22–23	
Romans 1:24	

12. Identify the exchange that has been made. Romans 1:23, 25

13. What disorder appears in Romans 1:26–28?

14. What does the Catholic Church teach about this behavior?

CCC 2357	
CCC 2358	
CCC 2359	

*Is there such a thing as "objective truth?" Explain.

15. List some sins found in Romans 1:29–30.

16. What results from unrepentant sin?

Galatians 5:21
CCC 1852

17. What bears witness to the truth? CCC 1777

18. How can sin become contagious? Romans 1:32

19. What remedy does Jesus offer for the sin problem? Mark 1:14–15

20. What remedy does the Church offer for sin? CCC 1421–1422

* What support groups are available for people who struggle with specific sins and addictions? How does the Church offer help to people with particular temptations?

CHAPTER 2

Righteous Judgment
Romans 2

For he will render to every man according to his works:
to those who by patience in well-doing seek for glory and honor and immortality,
he will give eternal life;
but for those who are factious and do not obey the truth,
but obey wickedness, there will be wrath and fury.
Romans 2:6–7

God's righteous judgment is perfect. Why does Romans Chapter 2 begin with the word "therefore?" It seems that Paul may have been in the middle of developing a thought when, centuries later, the Archbishop of Canterbury, Cardinal Stephen Langton (AD 1150–1228), divided the Bible into chapters, interrupting Paul's train of thought. Hence, it makes sense to backtrack a bit to recall Paul's previous assertion. Paul claimed that sinners were without excuse, because although they knew God's goodness, they refused to honor God and give thanks to Him. Sinners exchanged the truth of God for a lie, and became filled with all manner of wickedness (Romans 1:21, 25, 29.) But, time will tell, and God will judge.

Jesus said, *"Judge not, that you be not judged. For with the judgment you pronounce you will be judged, and the measure you give will be the measure you get"* (Matthew 7:1–2). Paul seems to elaborate on this exhortation given by Jesus in order to make a point. Sin is not simply a Gentile problem, but a Jewish problem as well. Sin, the universal scourge of humanity, is *everyone's* problem. Examining one's own conscience and behavior must precede passing judgment on another.

Sin involves a rejection of God. Sin is an offense against God, as well as a fault against reason, truth, and right conscience (CCC 1849). Sin is a failure to genuinely love God and to give Him the honor, praise, and thanksgiving that He is due. Human activity warrants divine retribution. If a person fails to respect his Creator, he enters into a downward cycle of contradiction and confusion. Human persons cannot reflect the glory of God placed in them, when images of idols replace God's image and likeness. In dishonoring God, man dishonors himself, for he loses his meaning and purpose in life, which is to reflect the glory of God.

Evangelism may be easier in a prison than in a country club. Most inmates readily realize that they are guilty and deserving of punishment. Convicts are serious sinners in desperate need of mercy and redemption. The fashionable country club set are also badly in need of God's mercy and salvation, but it may be much more difficult for them to fathom this truth. The temptation emerges to focus on the obvious sins of others, while hiding, rationalizing, or ignoring the sins in one's own life. Jesus saw the outward appearance of some of the Pharisees, who hid their filth and sin. He called them *whitewashed tombs. So you also outwardly appear righteous to men, but within you are full of hypocrisy and iniquity* (Matthew 23:28).

"Those other folks may be sinners, but not me!" Presumption involves the sin of overconfidence in God's mercy. The Jews are God's Chosen People, but that honor does not give the individual Jew a "Stay Out of Hell Free" card. With special privilege comes unique responsibility. Being chosen by God and knowing God's law demands obedience to God's law and good conduct. Humans judge imperfectly. But God sees the heart. God judges perfectly, and perfect justice comes at the particular judgment that each person will face on the day of his or her death.

Do you suppose, O man, that when you judge those who do such things and yet do them yourself, you will escape the judgment of God? (Romans 2:3). God desires the sinner to come to repentance. In this day of mass social media, the scandals of celebrities, politicians, and churchmen can reach every corner of the globe in minutes. What people have done in the darkness can suddenly come into the light. But some sins remain hidden in this life. Paul warns: *Do you not know that God's kindness is meant to lead you to repentance? But by your hard and impenitent heart you are storing up wrath for yourself on the day of wrath when God's righteous judgment will be revealed* (Romans 2:4–5). Some people accept God's grace and repent in this life, while others remain recalcitrant to their last breath.

God will judge justly. The day of wrath is coming when God will receive recompense for the atrocities perpetrated against Him. *The great day of the LORD is near, near and hastening fast; the sound of the day of the LORD is bitter, the mighty man cries aloud there. A day of wrath is that day, a day of distress and anguish, a day of ruin and devastation, a day of darkness and gloom, a day of clouds and thick darkness, a day of trumpet blast and battle cry against the fortified cities* (Zephaniah 1:14–16). The final judgment will take place at the Second Coming of the Lord, when Jesus will come in glory to judge the living and the dead (Matthew 24:30–31). Paul encourages the Jews and the Gentiles to deal with sin now, and prepare for the judgment of God. No one knows the day or the hour when the Lord will return. A word to the wise is sufficient—get right with God today!

For he [God] will render to every man according to his works: to those who by patience in well-doing seek for glory and honor and immortality, he will give eternal life; but for those who are factious and do not obey the truth, but obey wickedness, there will be wrath and fury (Romans 2:6–8). Behaviors have consequences, in this life and in the world to come. Obeying God's law surpasses knowing God's law. Believers must strive to persevere in faithfulness and good works.

Jesus Christ is the Savior of the world. No one can save himself or herself by doing good works. No one can earn or merit salvation. Faith is the free gift of God. Belonging to God's Chosen People is a privilege, but it is not an assurance of salvation. Elsewhere, Paul says: *For in Christ Jesus neither circumcision nor uncircumcision is of any avail, but faith working through love* (Galatians 5:6).

Give studious attention to the prophetic writings and they will lead you on a clearer path to escape the eternal punishment and to obtain the eternal good things of God. He who gave the mouth for speech and formed the ears for hearing and made eyes for seeing will examine everything and will judge justly, granting recompense to each according to merit. To those who seek immortality by the patient exercise of good works, He will give everlasting life, joy, peace, rest, and all good things, which neither eye has seen nor ear heard, nor has it entered into the heart of man. For the unbelievers and for the contemptuous, and for those who do not submit to the truth but assent to iniquity, when they have been involved in adulteries and fornications and homosexualities and avarice and in lawless idolatries, there will be wrath and indignation, tribulation and anguish: and in the end, such men as these will be detained in everlasting fire.

Saint Theophilus of Antioch (†AD 191), *To Autolycus, 1, 14*

God gave the Mosaic Law to the Jewish people. This great privilege cannot be overstated. A contemporary western woman moved to a foreign culture that had never embraced the Judeo-Christian ethic. She was stunned to learn that lying was common and marital fidelity was not honored, because the Ten Commandments had never been taught in that particular culture. It would be hard to imagine a culture that did not worship God, honor parents, respect life, speak the truth, uphold marriage, and protect the rights and goods of others. Mosaic Law is a huge blessing to the Jewish people and to Christians, as well. It has been said that no one breaks the Ten Commandments; rather you break yourself against them. The Law of Moses remains intact over thousands of years.

The Jews, and those who know the law, are held to that standard. God will judge Gentiles, who did not receive the law, by the law of nature. God's law is written on the hearts of all. *But this is the covenant which I will make with the house of Israel after those days, says the* LORD: *I will put my law within them, and I will write it upon their hearts; and I will be their God, and they shall be my people* (Jeremiah 31:33). Everyone has a conscience. Most people who have fallen into sin recall a time prior to sinning when a nagging thought or small voice warned against the behavior. Even without the Mosaic Law, people have an innate sense of right and wrong. Everyone knows, for example, that it is wrong to murder an innocent person.

Their thoughts will defend these unbelievers on the Day of Judgment, so that they will be punished more tolerably, because in some way they did naturally the things that are of the law, having the work of the law written in their hearts to this extent, that they did not do to others what they would not wish to endure. But even in this they were sinners, because being men without faith, they did not refer their works to that end to which they ought to have referred them.

Saint Augustine of Hippo (AD 354–430), *Against Julian 4, 3, 25*

Saint Augustine suggests that unbelievers may not be punished as severely as those who have been privileged to have the law. And yet, everyone is responsible to reflect and ponder the Source of all goodness. All creation points to the magnificence of God as Paul stressed earlier. Everyone is responsible to seek and to know God.

> Creation . . . is both good and a pattern of God's wisdom and power and love of mankind. . . . Hear what Paul says: *Ever since the creation of the world the invisible properties of God are seen, perceived in the things He has made.* For each of these, by which he speaks, declares that it leads us to the knowledge of God, that it makes us know the Master better.
> Saint John Chrysostom (AD 344–407), *Homilies on the Devil*, 2, 3

Practice what you preach. Paul confronts the Jews with the inconsistencies between their beliefs and their behaviors. There must be consistency between creed, cult, and conduct. One who preaches against idolatry must not have idols. If you teach others not to steal, do not steal. If you preach against adultery, do not commit adultery. *You who boast in the law, do you dishonor God by breaking the law* (Romans 2:23)? While Paul confronts the Jews, the same examination could be directed toward Christians. What kind of example does the believer give to unbelievers? Does the believer's behavior reflect his belief and honor God, or cause scandal?

Circumcision is a mark of honor for the Jew, a sign of the covenant between God and Abraham. Circumcision is an external sign of a spiritual, internal reality. In the Hebrew Scriptures, God spoke of a circumcision of the heart. *And the LORD your God will circumcise your heart and the heart of your offspring, so that you will love the LORD your God with all your heart and with all your soul, that you may live* (Deuteronomy 30:6). Later, Paul also speaks of a circumcision of the heart. *For we are the true circumcision, who worship God in spirit, and glory in Christ Jesus, and put no confidence in the flesh* (Philippians 3:3).

Bernard Nathanson, MD (1926–2001), a non-observant Jew, was once the most prominent abortionist in America. After having performed over 50,000 abortions, including the termination of his own child, he agreed to film an abortion using ultrasound technology for a friend. He watched in horror as the baby tried to evade his intrusive instrument of death. Bernard could find nothing in Judaism to help him deal with the enormous guilt he felt when he realized he was taking innocent human lives. He stopped doing abortions, but the magnitude of his sins overwhelmed him. A Catholic priest befriended Bernard and offered him books to read. In 1996, Cardinal John O'Connor baptized Bernard Nathanson in Saint Patrick's Cathedral in New York City. After the baptism, Cardinal O'Connor said, "Today, Bernard all your sins are forgiven. Now, you are as Catholic as I am." God's amazing mercy surpasses all the sins of all Jews and all Gentiles.

1. Use a dictionary to define the word "judgment."

2. What can you learn about judgment from these passages?

Matthew 7:1	
John 7:24	
Romans 2:1–2	
Romans 2:3	

3. For what is God waiting and hoping? Romans 2:4

4. In your own words, explain Romans 2:6–8.

5. What does Jesus say? Matthew 16:27

6. Compare the following verses.

2 Corinthians 5:10	
Revelation 22:12	

* How important is knowledge of Scripture versus obedience to Scripture?

7. What particular trait is evidenced below?

Romans 2:11
James 2:1–9

* How do you try not to show partiality to your children and grandchildren?

8. Put Romans 2:13 in your own words.

9. Where else has God placed His Law?

Jeremiah 31:33
Romans 2:15
Hebrews 8:8–11; 10:16

10. Use the Catechism of the Catholic Church to explain "conscience."

CCC 1776
CCC 1777
CCC 1778

* How can someone develop a well-formed conscience?

11. What will happen "on that day"?

Ecclesiastes 12:13–14
Romans 2:16
1 Corinthians 4:5
CCC 678

12. Why does a "day of wrath" approach? Zephaniah 1:14–17

13. How could you prepare for the "day of wrath?" Zephaniah 2:3

14. Of what does Paul accuse the teachers of the law? Romans 2:17–23

* How could this be a problem in contemporary society?

15. Identify some of the sins against the commandments Paul cites.

Exodus 20:1–3; Romans 2:22b
Exodus 20:14; Romans 2:22
Exodus 20:15; Romans 2:21

16. What can you learn from these verses?

Isaiah 52:5–6	
Romans 2:24	

17. How can a Christian counteract the blasphemy of God's Name? CCC 2814

18. When is circumcision of value? Romans 2:25–26

19. How can the uncircumcised please God? Romans 2:26–27

20. How does Paul describe a real Jew?

Romans 2:28–29	
Colossians 2:11–12	
Galatians 6:13–15	

* What practical thing can you do circumcise your heart for God?

CHAPTER 3

Redemption in Christ
Romans 3

Since all have sinned and fall short of the glory of God,
they are justified by his grace as a gift,
through the redemption which is in Christ Jesus,
whom God put forward as an expiation by his blood,
to be received by faith.
Romans 3:23–24

Paul continues his diatribe with an imaginary interlocutor, perhaps a faithful observant Jew. What is Paul's overall goal? Paul is trying to show that all people need redemption. Everyone needs a Savior. Imagine that a boat sinks in the middle of the ocean. A devout religious person and a murderer plunge into the sea, attempting to swim five hundred miles to the shore. Which person needs to be rescued more? Obviously, both of them need to be rescued. In a similar way, the chasm between sinful humanity and the perfect holiness of God is unimaginable.

For Paul to assert that all men, Jews and Gentiles, need redemption, he must level the playing field. He must transcend the division between Jews and pagans. Paul endeavors to equalize the difference between status and situation—the status of belonging to the Chosen People, and the situation of being a pagan. The election of the Jews is a privilege given for a purpose, a responsibility, not for boasting or superiority. Perhaps this chapter could be organized in the following way.

Romans 3	
Romans 3:1–8	God's faithfulness warrants the coherence of divine justice.
Romans 3:9–20	Man is to blame for sinful humanity, not God.
Romans 3:21–26	God has not abandoned His people, but manifests His justice in an unheard of new way.

Understanding Romans 3 requires a consideration of some literary devices:
    Allusion — an indirect reference to Sacred Scripture
    Hyperbole — exaggeration used to shock or make a significant point.

Jesus uses both of these literary devices in His sermons and parables. He frequently quotes Scripture, without citing the particular source. *"Have you not read that he who made them from the beginning made them male and female"* (Matthew 19:4), alludes to Genesis 1:27ff. When Jesus says, *"If your right eye causes you to sin, pluck it out and throw it away; it is better that you lose one of your members than that your whole body be thrown into hell"* (Matthew 5:29), Jesus does not mandate bodily mutilation. Rather, He exaggerates a point to urge listeners to deal seriously with sin, which has grave consequences. Keep this in mind when reading the Pauline letters.

The historical privilege of the Jews is manifested in that the Jews were the first people to hear the Word of God. God revealed Himself and spoke to Abraham (Genesis 12:1ff) and promised him descendants, land, and a blessing. *"I will bless those who bless you, and him who curses you I will curse; and by you all the families of the earth shall bless themselves"* (Genesis 12:3). The psalmist begs God, *keep me as the apple of the eye, hide me in the shadow of your wings* (Psalm 17:8). Moreover, God gave the Law to Moses, which proved a profound privilege that has benefitted humanity for thousands of years. Knowing and obeying God's Law enables people to live in harmony and brings peace among people.

What if some were unfaithful? Does their faithlessness nullify the faithfulness of God? By no means! Let God be true, though every man be false (Romans 3:3–4). God's Law remains good and useful, even when people fall short and disobey. But, even with the privilege of the Law, both Jews and non-Jews are under the dominion of sin. All are sons of Adam and daughters of Eve. Man's common inheritance is the plight of fallen humanity. Knowing God's Law is insufficient; privileged people are responsible to keep God's Law and be an example of righteous living.

The universal dominion of sin infects all of humanity. Does Paul mean to suggest that each and every person is guilty of sin, or that all people, both Jews and Gentiles sin? Obviously, each and every person cannot be guilty of sin. Jesus was like us in all things and was tempted, but never sinned. A child who dies in infancy has neither the capacity nor opportunity to sin. Nevertheless, Paul points out the universal pervasiveness of sin, using a *catena* (chain) of Scriptural allusions.

Ecclesiastes 7:20	*Surely there is not a righteous man on earth who does good and never sins.*
Psalm 14:1	*They are corrupt, they do abominable deeds, there is none that does good.*
Psalm 14:3	*They have all gone astray, they are all alike corrupt; there is none that does good, no, not one.*
Psalm 53:3	*They have all fallen away; they are all alike depraved; there is none that does good, no, not one.*
Psalm 140:3	*They make their tongue sharp as a serpent's, and under their lips is the poison of vipers.*
Psalm 5:9	*For there is no truth in their mouth; their heart is destruction, their throat an open sepulcher.*
Psalm 35:1	*Transgression speaks to the wicked deep in his heart, there is no fear of God before his eyes*
Isaiah 59:7	*Their feet run to evil, and they make haste to shed innocent blood.*

Paul accuses the whole human race of sinfulness, collectively implicating both Jew and Gentile in the miserable plight of humanity. Perhaps all you need to do is to read the morning newspaper to find similar evidence. The whole world must be accountable to God for disobedience and sinfulness. The pervasiveness of evil infects all people in all cultures on the planet. The law-abiding person longs to make an objection and to become an exception. *Let every mouth be stopped* (Romans 3:19) harkens back to the plight of Job protesting his innocence before God. *"Behold, I am of small account; what shall I answer you? I lay my hand on my mouth"* (Job 40:4). The most appropriate response for any human being before the perfect, supremely holy God is to shut one's mouth. Period. Silence.

Faith in Jesus Christ brings redemption for all sinners. *But now* indicates that Paul will transition into revealing the solution to this difficult problem and tenuous situation. *But now the righteousness of God has been manifested apart from law, although the law and the prophets bear witness to it, the righteousness of God through faith in Jesus Christ for all who believe* (Romans 3:21–22).

> Inasmuch as *[Christ]* gave Himself for the redemption of the whole human race, *[Paul]* said, as we have seen above, that He redeemed those who were bound in the captivity of their sins, when, separate from God, He tasted death for all.
> Origen (AD 185–254), *Commentaries on Romans, 3, 8*

For there is no distinction; since all have sinned and fall short of the glory of God, they are justified by his grace as a gift, through the redemption which is in Christ Jesus, whom God put forward as an expiation by his blood, to be received by faith (Romans 3:22b–25). Faithful Jews believed that they could become righteous by remaining completely obedient to the law. Grace, the free and undeserved gift of God, enables a person to recognize his or her need for redemption. Faith is a gift of God, a human response to the grace that enables a person to assent to the fullness of truth that God has revealed. Grace and faith enable a person to be justified, through Christ, and become a child of God.

Justification

The grace of the Holy Spirit has the power to justify us, to cleanse us from our sins and to communicate to us "the righteousness of God through faith in Jesus Christ" and through Baptism—the sanctification and renewal of the inner man. CCC 1987

Justification not only removes our sins, but also enables sanctification and the renewal of one's soul. In 1547, the Council of Trent explained that justification transitions a person from being a child of Adam to the state of grace and adoption as a child of God, through the merits of the new Adam—Jesus Christ. However, in order to obtain the grace of justification, a person must first acknowledge that he or she has a *need* to be redeemed and justified. The gift cannot be given to someone who does not want or need it. You cannot earn salvation; it is a gift for sinners.

> Let no one say to himself: "If [justification] is from faith, how is it freely given: If faith merits it, why is it not rather paid than given?" Let the faithful man not say such a thing; for, if he says: "I have faith, therefore I merit justification," he will be answered: "What have you that you did not receive?" If, therefore, faith entreats and receives justification, according as God has apportioned to each in the measure of his faith, nothing of human merit precedes the grace of God, but grace itself merits increase, and the increase merits perfection, with the will accompanying but not leading, following along but not going in advance.
>
> Saint Augustine of Hippo (AD 354–430),
> *Letter of Augustine to Paulinus of Nola, 186, 3, 10*

God has given us what we could never have achieved for ourselves. Salvation is from the Jews. However, salvation does not come from Israel's law, but from Israel's Messiah, the Son of David. Paul encourages us not to overthrow or ignore the law, but to uphold the law. The law is holy, righteous, and good, and yet the law is powerless in enabling people to fulfill its demands, given fallen human nature. Despite the goodness of the law, people need grace and faith to become obedient to the Lawgiver. Jesus Christ, the Son of God, models perfect obedience to the law. And, in so doing, He provides the means for our redemption and justification.

Rosalind Moss was one of three children raised in a conservative, observant Jewish family in Brooklyn, New York. Every year, her parents set an empty place at the Seder Dinner table for the Prophet Elijah. Every year, she heard the Passover story recounted again, and prayed the familiar prayers.

When she was thirty-two years old, Rosalind heard about Jesus Christ for the first time from her older brother David, who belongs to the Association of Hebrew Catholics. Rosalind said, "You mean to tell me that the Messiah was already here? He was the only hope the world ever had, and yet the Jewish people didn't know this? That is insanity!" And yet, at the Easter Vigil in 1995, Rosalind Moss accepted the grace of God and became a Catholic. Subsequently, she discerned a religious vocation and became Mother Miriam of the Lamb of God, OSB. She is the foundress of the Daughters of Mary, Mother of Our Hope, in Tulsa, Oklahoma.

Perhaps the example of Mother Miriam illustrates how difficult it was in Paul's time, and still is today, for people to acknowledge their need for redemption, and to recognize Jesus Christ, the Jewish Messiah and Savior of the whole world.

1. What can you learn from these verses?

Psalm 147:19–20
Romans 3:1–2

2. Explain an essential characteristic of God from these sources.

Romans 3:3–4
CCC 2465

3. What can you learn about "truth?"

CCC 2466
CCC 2467
CCC 2469

4. Humanity is under the power of what?

Romans 3:9
CCC 1849
CCC 1850

5. What is necessary for salvation?

Psalm 51:1–4
CCC 1847

6. How can you explain Romans 3:10–12?

7. Can you think of an exception to Romans 3:10? Luke 1:5–6; 2:25

8. Explain some sins described in Romans 3:13–14.

9. Compare the following verses.

Tobit 14:1–2
Romans 3:18

* Think of a contemporary righteous, God-fearing person you know.

10. What can you learn from these verses? Job 40:4–5; Romans 3:19

11. Compare the following verses.

Acts 13:38–39	
Romans 3:20	

12. Describe the righteousness of God.

Romans 3:21	
CCC 2542	
CCC 2543	

13. Use a dictionary to define "righteousness."

14. How can you get the righteousness of God? Romans 3:22

15. What happens when man sins?

Romans 3: 23	
CCC 705	

* How do you feel when you sin?

16. Use a dictionary or the Catechism to define "justification." CCC 1990

17. How is one justified?

Romans 3:23–26
1 John 2:1–2
CCC 1992

18. For whom did Jesus come?

Acts 10:34–35
Romans 3:28

19. Does the law have any merit?

Joshua 1:7–8
Psalm 119:1
Sirach 2:15–16

20. Does Paul intend to disregard the Law? Romans 3:31

* Do you think it is helpful to teach the Ten Commandments today?

CHAPTER 4

Abraham's Faith
Romans 4

The promise to Abraham and his descendants,
that they should inherit the world,
did not come through the law
but through the righteousness of faith.
Romans 4:13

The example of the faith of father Abraham inspires all people, Jews as well as non-Jews. Paul attempts to prove that Abraham believed, and was considered righteous by God, while he was still a pagan, before he was circumcised. In so doing, Paul will suggest that Abraham, the father of the Chosen People, can also be seen as the father of all who believe in God. Abraham passes on his physical heritage to the Jewish people and his spiritual heritage to all people of faith.

Abraham was the friend of God (Isaiah 41:8). The Chronicler asks, *"Did you not, O our God, drive out the inhabitants of this land before your people Israel, and give it forever to the descendants of Abraham your friend* (2 Chronicles 20:7). Why is Abraham God's friend? Was Abraham God's friend because he was faithful to God? Or was Abraham God's friend simply because God chose him and blessed him?

Romans 4	
Romans 4:1–12	Abraham believes God and is justified.
Romans 4:13–25	God's promise is realized through believing.

Faith is both a free gift from God and a human decision enabled by the same grace, by which a person believes God and gives assent to the fullness of truth that God has revealed. The basis of faith is the word of God. Only God's word can provide man his identity. In Abraham's act of faith, observe two actions.

    1) The word of God invites Abraham to trust.
    2) The word of man (Abraham) gives his assent to God.

This double movement of faith can also be found in the Incarnation. The Angel Gabriel presents the word of God to the Virgin Mary with an invitation to trust (Luke 1:26–31). The Virgin Mary believes and gives her assent to God, *"Behold, I am the handmaid of the Lord; let it be to me according to your word"* (Luke 1:38). The Blessed Mother's amazing faith surpasses that of Abraham.

The law is incapable of manifesting the origin, purpose, and future of man. The law is good and has a place and function in the economy of salvation. But the law is not the defining place of faith, where one gives assent to God in his initial conversion. Paul uses the term "law" in a special way. He speaks of law as a theological system in which fulfilling the law determines the fate of man, in other words, legalism. Paul quotes the psalmist (Psalm 32:1–2; Romans 4:7–8) to reveal that righteousness and blessedness are evidenced in the life of Abraham. In this beatitude, God asks nothing of a person but to believe and to trust in Him.

Righteousness	Blessedness
Genesis 15:16	Psalm 32:1–2
God	God
reckoned	did not reckon (impute)
it (the faith)	the sin
of Abraham	of man

Abraham's faith became the basis for his righteousness. Blessedness (grace) is the free gift of God, enabling justification. Justification involves conversion. 1) Hear the gospel, 2) believe in the word of life, and 3) grace opens the heart to God. God's merciful act of forgiving the believer's sins enables him to be justified. While sin remains an objective fact, a reality that may be recorded in history, God chooses to pardon the repentant sinner. God's mercy extends beyond human comprehension, and certainly surpasses the expectation of retribution that the people of Paul's time expect. *For as the heavens are high above the earth, so great is his mercy toward those who fear him; as far as the east is from the west, so far does he remove our transgressions from us* (Psalm 103:11–12).

Righteousness apart from works, in Paul's Letter to the Romans, refers specifically to the moment of conversion—that event in which one becomes a believer. Works of the law include circumcision and obedience to prescribed directives, which are good, but cannot achieve what only God can give—redemption. The apostle James says something quite different. *What does it profit, my brethren, if a man says he has faith, but has not works? . . . But some will say, "You have faith and I have works." Show me your faith apart from your works, and I by my works will show you my faith* (James 2:14, 18). James assumes that the believer has already been freely justified. For James, if faith is genuine it must produce the evidence of faith. Ethics becomes the privileged locus for the verification of faith. James considers the believer in his daily life. If one is a son or daughter of God, he or she must take a concern for the brothers and sisters (James 2:15). Perhaps James admonishes lazy Christians, who sit around waiting for Jesus to come again in glory, while Paul speaks to those who have yet to encounter the Lord and experience conversion.

Circumcision is the sign of the covenant between God and His people. *"This is my covenant, which you shall keep, between me and you and your descendants after you: Every male among you shall be circumcised* (Genesis 17:10). Circumcision is a good thing, a sign of honor, a mark of the covenant between God and His Chosen People. Circumcision is a physical reminder of God's promises to Abraham. Paul recalls that God chose Abraham out of nowhere, and made promises to him, even while Abraham was still a pagan, and before he was circumcised. Abraham had faith before he was circumcised and before he saw the promises fulfilled.

God's promise to Abraham was threefold—blessings, descendants, and land. God promised to make Abraham's name great and to make him a great nation. Abraham would be blessed and would be a blessing to others. His descendants would be as numerous as the stars in the sky. Abraham would be given the Promised Land.

    1) *I will make of you a great nation, and I will bless you, and make your name great, so that you will be a blessing. I will bless those who bless you . . . and by you all the families of the earth shall bless themselves* (Genesis 12:2–3).

    2) *To your descendants I give this land, from the river of Egypt to the great river, the river Euphrates* (Genesis 15:18).

    3) *You shall be the father of a multitude of nations* (Genesis 17:4).

However, Abraham had a huge problem. He was an old man, one hundred years old. And Abraham's wife Sarah was ninety, far past her childbearing years. Paul recalls the predicament of Abraham and Sarah. *He did not weaken in faith when he considered his own body, which was as good as dead because he was about a hundred years old, or when he considered the barrenness of Sarah's womb. No distrust made him waver concerning the promise of God, but he grew strong in his faith as he gave glory to God, fully convinced that God was able to do what he promised* (Romans 4:19–21). Faith opens up a future, a promise of life and continuity. Only by faith can a believer enter into that fecundity.

Abraham believes that God, *who gives life to the dead and calls into existence the things that do not exist* (Romans 4:17), will also overcome the dead-ness of his own body and the barrenness of Sarah's womb. God promises. Abraham believes, and trusts God. *That is why his faith was "reckoned to him as righteousness"* (Romans 4:23). God proposes, and Abraham believes, and receives all—his identity as a father, his sons as his posterity, his blessing, his land, his nation, and his greatness. Moreover, Abraham is not just the father of one nation, the nation of Israel—he is the father of "many nations." Faith allows non-Jews to enter into the family as sons and daughters of God. The faith of Abraham was manifest long before he saw the fulfillment of the promise. God gives that gift of faith to people of all nations.

> **Justification** — the repentant sinner, by the mercy of God, through the sacrifice of Christ, by means of sanctifying grace, becomes right with God through baptism.

Just as God overcame the dead-ness of Abraham and Sarah's infertility, God transcended the dead-ness of Jesus Christ in the tomb, and *raised from the dead Jesus our Lord, who was put to death for our trespasses and raised for our justification* (Romans 4:24–25). Abraham put his faith in God alone (Romans 4:3). Christians put total faith in the One God who raised Jesus from the dead (Romans 4:24). Paul connects faith in God to the Christ event. Because Jesus suffered, died, and is risen, Christian faith involves believing in God who freely justifies us through Jesus Christ. Faith is now inseparable from that spectacular event.

> "He was handed over for our offenses, and He rose again for our justification." What does that mean, "for our justification?" So that He might justify us; so that He might make us just. For it is better that you be just than that you be a man. If God made you a man, and you made yourself just, something you were doing would be better than what God did. But God made you without any cooperation on your part. For you did not lend your consent so that God could make you. How could you have consented, when you did not exist? But He who made you without your consent does not justify you without your consent. He made you without your knowledge, but He does not justify you without your willing it.
> Saint Augustine of Hippo (AD 354–430), *Sermons 169, 13*

Paul provides a wonderful reflection on the faith of Abraham. The true example of Abraham's faith consists in remaining steadfast, trusting in God, despite his apparent dead-ness and the hopelessness of his situation. Christians too should find hope in their situations of "dead-ness," for whatever the situation, it will always be characterized by suffering, persecution, and death. But, glory be to God in Jesus Christ, who conquered sin and death, once and for all, in His Resurrection.

> John Riccardo, a typical college graduate, disenchanted with life, heard God call him, like Abraham, out of nowhere. God called John to be a priest when he was not even faithfully attending Sunday Mass. However, grace and faith change things. Father John Riccardo obeyed God's call, studied in Rome, and did graduate study on Ephesians at the Pontifical John Paul II Institute for studies on Marriage and the Family. He now hosts the Catholic radio program *Christ Is the Answer* on EWTN.

1. What can you say about Abraham?

Romans 4:1–4
Hebrews 11:8–12
CCC 146

2. Compare and explain the following verses.

Romans 4:2
James 2:14–18

* Can you earn your salvation?

3. How does one achieve righteousness? Psalm 32:1–2; Romans 4:6–8

4. When was Abraham justified? Romans 4:9–10

5. Explain this command of God. Genesis 17:9–11

6. What is the significance of circumcision? Romans 4:11–12

7. Who are the children of Abraham? Romans 4:11–12, 16

8. How did God fulfill His promise? Romans 4:13, CCC 706

9. In your own words, explain Romans 4:15.

10. What three things did God promise Abraham? Genesis 12:1–3; 17:6–8

11. What does Sirach reveal about Abraham? Sirach 44:19–21

12. What does God do? Romans 4:17

13. How and what did Abraham believe? Romans 4:18

14. Define "hope." CCC 1817

15. Why was Abraham troubled? Romans 4:19

* Have you ever faced a hopeless situation? What did you do?

16. What reckons Abraham righteous? Romans 4:21–22

17. What reckons believers righteous?

Romans 4:23–25
CCC 517

18. What did Jesus do for humanity? Romans 4:25

19. How can you be united to Christ? CCC 977

20. Define faith and list some biblical examples of faith.

Hebrews 11:1
Sirach 44–45
Sirach 46–48
Hebrews 11:4–7, 23–28

* Share some contemporary examples of strong faith.

Monthly Social Activity

This month, your small group will meet for coffee, tea, or a simple breakfast, lunch, or dessert in someone's home. Pray for this social event and for the host or hostess. Try, if at all possible, to attend.

Just to help the members of your small group get to know you better, write down two true things about yourself, and one false thing. Do not put your name on the paper. At the social gathering, all papers will be pulled out and read. Guess which person is described and identify the false statement.

Some examples:

* ❧ *I am a gourmet cook. I speak French. I don't drive.*

* ❧ *I play golf. I play bridge. I go to daily Mass.*

* ❧ *I won a scholarship. I am an only child. I have four children*

CHAPTER 5

Jesus, the New Adam
Romans 5

If, because of one man's trespass, death reigned through that one man,
much more will those who receive the abundance of grace
and the free gift of righteousness
reign in life through the one man Jesus Christ.
Romans 5:17

Therefore signals a transition, or a shift from the problem of sin experienced by both Jews and Gentiles to the solution—a new hope, offered by God in giving His Son—Jesus Christ, for the salvation of the world. Paul presents a concentric schema of thought that is framed by hope, beginning in Romans 5:1–21 and ending in Romans 8:14–39. *Therefore, since we are justified by faith, we have peace with God through our Lord Jesus Christ. Through him we have obtained access to this grace in which we stand, and we rejoice in our hope of sharing the glory of God* (Romans 5:1–2). *For in this hope we were saved* (Romans 8:24).

Romans 5:3–5

We rejoice in our sufferings, knowing that
    suffering → produces → endurance
      endurance → produces → character
        character → produces → hope,
          and hope does not disappoint us,
because God's love has been poured into our hearts through the Holy Spirit.

Hope does not disappoint us; it does not allow believers to be left in despair and shame, as the Psalmist prays: *To you they cried, and were saved; in you they trusted and were not disappointed* (Psalm 22:5). *O my God, in you I trust, let me not be put to shame; let not my enemies exult over me. Yes, let none that wait for you be put to shame* (Psalm 25:2). Hope comes from peace with God, which comes from justification, and of which the Spirit gives witness.

Faith, hope, and love—the theological virtues emerge at the beginning of Romans 5.

> ➤ *since we are justified by **faith*** (Romans 5:1)
> ➤ *we rejoice in our **hope** of sharing the glory of God* (Romans 5:2b)
> ➤ *because God's **love** has been poured into our hearts* (Romans 5:5).

Christians habitually practice and display these theological virtues in their daily lives. If these three theological virtues are absent in the life of Christians, how is it possible to be a light to the world, or to hope to evangelize others?

Peace transcends emotional tranquility—peace involves right relationship with God. Christian hope remains strong, even in suffering. Because Christ was crucified, His people must be cruciform. The Christian embraces suffering and joins his or her suffering to that of Christ. The Christian who hopes for glory must pass by way of the cross—*through many tribulations we must enter the kingdom of God* (Acts 14:22b). Catholic theology offers the consolation of redemptive suffering.

God's love has been poured into our hearts through the Holy Spirit who has been given to us (Romans 5:5). Jesus promised that the Father would send the Holy Spirit to the faithful: *the Holy Spirit, whom the Father will send in my name, he will teach you all things* (John 14:26). Even the prophets foretold this amazing gift. *I will pour my Spirit upon your descendants, and my blessing on your offspring* (Isaiah 44:3b). *And it shall come to pass afterward, that I will pour out my spirit on all flesh; your sons and your daughters shall prophesy, your old men shall dream dreams, and your young men shall see visions* (Joel 2:28). The promised Holy Spirit has now come and dwells in the hearts of Christian believers.

Paul explains the amazing gift of God. *But God shows his love for us in that while we were yet sinners Christ died for us* (Romans 5:8). Jesus explained the significance of His sacrifice prior to His death. *"Greater love has no man than this, that a man lay down his life for his friends* (John 15:13). Saint Peter expounded upon this truth: *For Christ also died for sins once for all, the righteous for the unrighteous, that he might bring us to God, being put to death in the flesh but made alive in the spirit* (1 Peter 3:18). The beloved disciple, Saint John, exhorts, *by this we know love, that he laid down his life for us; and we ought to lay down our lives for the brethren* (1 John 3:16). The blood of Christ effects our justification before the Father.

But what better reason is there for the coming of Christ, than that God might show His love among us, and how very great that love is, for when we were still his enemies, Christ died for us? But this was done also, since the end of the commandment and the fullness of the law is love, so that we might love one another and lay down our life for the brethren just as He laid down His life for us; and in regard to God Himself, if before it were tedious to love Him, now at least it will not be tedious; because God first loved us and did not spare His only Son, but delivered Him up for us. For there is no greater invitation to being loved than to offer one's own love first. The Lord Jesus Christ, the God-man, is both a manifestation of divine love in us, and an example of human humility among us, so that our great pride might be healed by an even greater contrary medicine. For a proud man is a great misery; but a humble God is a greater mercy.
Saint Augustine of Hippo (AD 354–430), *Rudimentary Catechesis, 4, 7*

By means of a Jewish "*a fortiori* argument" (Latin: with stronger reason) following the logic that a point is proven from a previously established fact or a stronger claim, Paul counters the fear of judgment. If God declared that we, who were guilty and deserving of His wrath, are innocent (justified), how much more will He declare us, who are now justified (innocent) at the Last Judgment (Romans 5:9)? So the initial premise provides the logical assumption for the second premise.

In a second "*a fortiori* argument," Paul jumps to a higher level of thought, with a more mystical model. We are reconciled by the death of Christ, so shall we be saved by Christ's life. *For if while we were enemies we were reconciled to God by the death of his Son, much more, now that are reconciled, shall we be saved by his life* (Romans 5:10). By the *death* of Jesus, we have the hope of eternal *life*.

The Theology of Participation emerges in Romans. If the Christian *dies with Christ* in Baptism, he or she will hope to *rise with Christ* in His Resurrection. The believer must repent and put to death the old man, the sinful nature, in order to accept the grace to believe, to be saved, and to put on Christ the divine nature.

> When we are baptized, we are enlightened. Being enlightened, we are adopted as sons. Adopted as sons, we are made perfect. Made perfect, we become immortal. . . . This work is variously called grace, illumination, perfection, and washing. It is a washing by which we are cleansed of sins; a gift of grace by which the punishments due our sins are remitted; an illumination by which we behold that holy light of salvation—that is, by which we see God clearly; and we call that perfection which leaves nothing lacking. Indeed, if a man know God, what more does he need? Certainly it were out of place to call that which is not complete a true gift of God's grace. Because God is perfect, the gifts He bestows are perfect.
>
> Saint Clement of Alexandria (AD 150–216),
> *The Instructor of Children*, 1, 6, 26

Jesus, the New Adam appears as a typological antithesis. Whereas Adam brought death into the world through his disobedience to God, Jesus triumphs over sin and death, and brings life by His perfect obedience to the Father. Jesus conquers death in His Resurrection on Easter morning. Jesus brings humankind the hope of eternal life. Adam and Eve's sin of disobedience brought original sin and death to their descendants, leaving people spiritually impoverished. The original grace and holiness that Adam and Eve enjoyed vanished, replaced by original sin. Jesus, the New Adam, brings new life, grace, and the free gift of righteousness.

Paul must make two corrections in his parallelism. The first correction involves sin and death. Sin existed before the law was given, but it was not reckoned. That is why Adam is only an image of the New Man to come. Therefore, this is a limited form of parallelism. The second correction involves New Life. The life which Christ brought to us, in which we partake, is entirely much more rich and abundant than natural life. The New Life in Christ Jesus brings divine life and the hope of eternal life into the repentant believer. New Life far surpasses natural human life.

A		Romans 5:12	**Adam**	
	B	Romans 5:13–17		**Law**
A*		Romans 5:18–19	**Christ**	

The Legacy of Christ unfolds in Paul's preaching. In Greek, the word "because" indicates a conditional relationship or clause, similar to those in a legal contract. Person A receives from Person B a legacy or benefit, provided that Person A has met the legal requirement in fulfilling the predetermined condition.

> We partake in the legacy of Adam
> *because* (we fulfilled the clause) — we sinned.
>
> We will partake in the legacy of Christ
> *because* (we fulfill the clause) — we believe.

Paul closes this chapter by asserting that *where sin increased, grace abounded all the more, so that, as sin reigned in death, grace also might reign through righteousness to eternal life through Jesus Christ our Lord* (Romans 5:20–21). Anyone who has been at the bottom of his barrel, without hope, and finds Christ can testify to the truth of these words. The dramatic conversion of sinners into saints, in history and in contemporary times, proves that God's grace continues to pour forth.

Joseph Pearce, alone in a bleak London prison cell just before Christmas in 1985, experienced the darkest day of his life. Sentenced to a year's imprisonment for inciting racial hatred, this was not his first incarceration. Joseph's anti-Catholicism, learned at this father's knee, had deepened and darkened with his involvement in terrorist organizations in Northern Ireland. Surprisingly, during his trial, someone handed Joseph a rosary. Even though he didn't know any prayers or the mysteries of the rosary, he began to fumble the beads and mumble something. It was the first time in his life that he had ever tried to pray. The results were nothing short of astonishing as the eyes of faith began to open, and a hand of healing began to soften his hardened heart. God's grace was overwhelming. He began to read G. K. Chesterton, and on Saint Joseph's Day 1989, at the age of twenty-eight, Joseph Pearce was received into the arms of Holy Mother Church. A merciful God had embraced yet another prodigal son, who would go on to become a prolific Catholic author, distinguished professor, and beloved speaker.

1. What hope does the justified believer have? Romans 5:1–2

2. How does one discern how to deal with suffering and trials?

Acts 14:22
Romans 5:3
James 1:2
CCC 2847

3. In your own words, explain "redemptive suffering." James 5:10–13

4. What can you learn about the virtue of hope?

Psalm 42:5, 11
Psalm 119:116
Romans 5:4–5
CCC 2090

5. Explain Philippians 1:20 in your own words.

6. Use a dictionary or the Catechism to define hope. CCC 1817

7. What happens in these verses?

Acts 2:1–4
Acts 2:33
Romans 5:5

8. What can you learn about love?

Romans 5:5–8
1 John 4:8, 16
CCC 733

9. Compare the following verses.

John 15:13
Romans 5:8
1 Peter 3:18
1 John 3:16; 4:10

10. What did God do for humanity?

Romans 5:9–11
1 Thessalonians 1:10

11. How did sin come into the world? Genesis 3:1–7

12. How do people fall into sin? James 1:13–15

* Share some of the temptations you encounter and how to avoid them.

13. Identify one of the punishments of sin.

Genesis 3:19
Romans 5:12

*When do you hear "from dust you came and to dust you shall return?"

14. What is the consequence of sin? CCC 1008

15. In your own words, explain Romans 5:13–14.

16. How are people saved? Acts 15:11

Acts 15:11
Romans 5:15–16

17. How is death transformed?

Romans 5:17
CCC 1009

18. Which two people are referenced in Romans 5:19?

19. Find the promise in Romans 5:20b.

20. By what means can grace reign? Romans 5:21

* Which verse challenged you the most in this lesson?

Chapter 6

The Legacy of Christ
Romans 6

Do you not know that all of us who have been baptized into Christ Jesus
were baptized into his death?
We were buried therefore with him by baptism into death,
so that as Christ was raised from the dead by the glory of the Father,
we too might walk in the newness of life.
Romans 6:3–4

Paul presents some interesting rhetorical questions to clarify his perspective. *What shall we say then? Are we to continue in sin that grace may abound* (Romans 6:1)? *What then? Are we to sin because we are not under law but under grace* (Romans 6:15)? He answers both questions emphatically: *By no means! How can we who died to sin still live in it* (Romans 6:2, 15b)? Root out sin at all cost.

Dying and rising with Christ—occurs in the sacrament of baptism, which enables moral transformation. In the sacrament of baptism, God pours forth grace to live a new way of life. *Do you not know that all of us who have been baptized into Christ Jesus were baptized into his death? We were buried therefore with him by baptism into death, so that as Christ was raised from the dead by the glory of the Father, we too might walk in the newness of life* (Romans 6:3–4). In baptism, the believer gives his life to Christ and is incorporated into the body of Christ, the Church.

> Israel was baptized in the midst of the sea on that Passover night, on the day of salvation; and our Savior washed the feet of His disciples on the Passover night—which is the Sacrament of Baptism. And you knew already, my beloved, that until this night when the Savior instituted true Baptism and when He conferred it upon His disciples, the baptism with which the priests were baptizing was that baptism of which John said: "Do penance for your sins." And on that night of His passion and death He showed them the Sacrament of Baptism, just as the Apostle has stated: "You have been buried with Him in Baptism unto death, and you have risen up with Him in the power of God." Know then, my beloved, that the baptism of John was of no value for the forgiveness of sins, but for repentance.
>
> Aphraates the Persian Sage (AD 280–345), *Treatises, 12, 10*

Noah's ark prefigured baptism, as God saved one family through the flood. Moses leading the people of Israel through the parted waters of the Red Sea to freedom prefigured the sacrament of baptism, as well. In baptism, the believer is plunged into the water, as Christ was plunged into death, and then the newly baptized emerges from the water, as Christ emerged alive from the tomb. The baptismal formula is Trinitarian: "I baptize you in the name of the Father, and of the Son, and of the Holy Spirit." The Catholic Church recognizes as validly baptized anyone who has been baptized with water and these words. Through baptism the believer is freed from sin and sacramentally assimilated into Jesus, who in His own baptism anticipated His death and Resurrection (CCC 537). In baptism, the believer renounces sin; strives to imitate Christ; conforms one's thoughts, words, and deeds to His; and is empowered by grace to walk in the newness of life.

God frees us from original sin in baptism. The death of Christ on the cross negates all self-sufficiency and pride. In a certain way the believer "cannot" sin anymore. The theology of retribution is pierced on the cross. Since the sin-less Jesus died on the cross, no one can consider present suffering as a punishment for sin or wealth as a sign of righteousness and blessing. On the one hand, sin (understood as self-sufficiency, trying to be saved without God) is no longer possible. On the other hand, sin (understood as moral failure) is still possible.

Being-in-Christ

Sin → *self-sufficiency, trying to save oneself without God* → is impossible.

Sin → *moral weakness and failure* → is still possible.

In baptism, God gives actual grace and sanctifying grace. So the Christian now has the power to resist the temptation to sin. However, God also gives each person free will. So even though the grace to resist sin is sufficient, the believer has the free will to accept the grace of God or to reject it. The Christian life remains a battlefield between good and evil until the end. *So you must also consider yourselves dead to sin and alive to God in Christ Jesus* (Romans 6:11).

You have a choice. *Let not sin therefore reign in your mortal bodies, to make you obey their passions* (Romans 6:12). Even with faith and baptism, Satan tempts. Peter gives a sober warning. *Be watchful. Your adversary the devil prowls around like a roaring lion, seeking some one to devour. Resist him, firm in your faith* (1 Peter 5:8–9). James offers similar advice. *Submit yourselves therefore to God. Resist the devil and he will flee from you. Draw near to God and he will draw near to you* (James 4:7–8). Look to Jesus for grace to stand firm in temptation.

Choose to be under the law or grace. Paul refers to the law as a theological system—a type of legalism—in which fulfilling the law determines one's ultimate fate. God's law is good and for our benefit. But the law lacks the power to enable us to be perfectly obedient and pleasing to God. Instead of being the solution to our troubles, the law merely reveals and highlights our transgressions. God's grace is central. Good works are a fruit of the Spirit (Galatians 5:22–23). Whoever tries to control his or her destiny by fulfilling the law is actually under the law. The Christian believes and trusts Christ for salvation, not the law.

The true believer, aware of being a sinner, aspires with his whole self—spirit, heart and body—to divine forgiveness, as to a new creation that can restore joy and hope to him (Psalm 51:3, 5, 12, 14) . . .

It is a spiritual battle waged against sin and finally against Satan. It is a struggle that involves the whole of the person and demands attentive and constant watchfulness.

Saint Augustine remarks that those who want to walk with the love of God and his mercy cannot be content with ridding themselves of grave and mortal sins *[only]*, but "should do the truth, also recognizing sins that are less grave . . . and come to the light by doing worthy actions. Even less grave sins, if they are ignored, proliferate and produce death."

Pope Benedict XVI, *Ash Wednesday Homily, 1 March 2006*

Christ liberates the believer in order to serve. Paul uses the imagery of slavery, which was very prevalent in the world at that time. A slave belonged to one master, and he could only work for and serve that master. Jesus also used the imagery of slavery to make a point. *"No one can serve two masters; for either he will hate the one and love the other, or he will be devoted to one and despise the other"* (Matthew 6:24). A slave can only be liberated when another master buys him.

Do you not know that if you yield yourselves to any one as obedient slaves, you are slaves of the one whom you obey, either of sin, which leads to death, or of obedience, which leads to righteousness? But thanks be to God, that you who were once slaves of sin have become obedient from the heart to the standard of teaching to which you were committed, and having been set free from sin, have become slaves of righteousness (Romans 6:16–18). A Christian serves only Christ. Jesus has set the believer free from sin. Sin no longer has mastery over him. Christ is now the Lord and Master. But unlike the slave, who has no choice, the believer has the choice to be faithful to his Master or to return to sin and become enslaved again.

Conflict continues in the human life. Jesus explains the tension of the spiritual battle. *"When the unclean spirit has gone out of a man, he passes through waterless places seeking rest, but he finds none. Then he says, 'I will return to my house from which I came.' And when he comes he finds it empty, swept, and put in order. Then he goes and brings with him seven other spirits more evil than himself, and they enter and dwell there"* (Matthew 12:43–45). Nature does not tolerate a void. It fills the void with something, either good or evil. A person cannot belong to no one. Self-love is so strong that when a believer stops loving God, he falls back on himself. Only when the Stronger One—Jesus—comes, who can draw him away from his egoistic circle, can a person be liberated from himself.

The temptation to organize the world and one's own life without God or even in opposition to God, without his commandments and without the Gospel, is a very real temptation and threatens us too. When human life and the world are built without God, they will eventually turn against man himself. Breaking the divine commandments, abandoning the path traced out for us by God, means falling into the slavery of sin, and *the wages of sin is death* (Romans 6:23).

We find ourselves face to face with the reality of sin. Sin is an offence against God, it is being disobedient to him, to his law, to the moral norms which God has given to man, inscribing them on the human heart, confirming and perfecting them by revelation. Sin pits itself against God's love for us and turns our hearts away from him. Sin is "love of self carried to the point of contempt for God," as Saint Augustine put it. Sin is a great evil in all its many dimensions. Starting with original sin, to the personal sins committed by each person, to social sins, the sins which weigh heavily on the history of the entire human family.

We must be constantly aware of this great evil; we must constantly cultivate the subtle sensitivity and clear consciousness of the seeds of death contained in sin. This is what is commonly known as the sense of sin. Its source is to be found in man's moral conscience; it is linked to the knowledge of God, to the experience of union with the Creator, Lord and Father. The more profound this awareness of union with God—strengthened by a person's sacramental life and by sincere prayer—the clearer the sense of sin is. The reality of God lays open and sheds light on the mystery of man. We must do all that we can to make our consciences more sensitive, and to guard them from becoming deformed or imperceptive.

We see what great tasks God has put before us. We must truly form our humanity in the image and likeness of God, to become people who love the law of God and want to live according to it.

Pope (Saint) John Paul II, *Homily, 6 June 1999.*

Paul illustrates the choice placed before each person. Slaves to sin experience bondage in this life and eternal damnation in the next. Servants of God enjoy peace, love, and joy in this life and hope for eternal bliss. *But the free gift of God is eternal life in Christ Jesus our Lord* (Romans 6:23b). Choose life. Choose Christ.

Dion DiMucci, *The Wanderer,* left home in the Bronx and found that hell is real. Rock and roll music brought fame and fortune, along with addictions to alcohol and drugs. Dion's wife Susan prayed to God for her husband's deliverance. And the power of God's love, the grace from receiving Christ's sacraments, and the support of others have enabled Dion to live in freedom for over four decades. Dion's life reveals the transforming power of Christ's love, *Love Came to Me.*

1. Explain the questions and answers in Romans 6:1–2 and 6:15.

2. What can you learn about baptism?

Matthew 28:19
Romans 6:3–5
CCC 1214
CCC 1215
CCC 1216
CCC 1227

* When were you baptized? What do you know about that day?

3. What happens to the believer in these verses?

Romans 6:5
CCC 790

4. What did Saint Peter recommend to the people on Pentecost? Acts 2:38

5. What happens in baptism?

CCC 537
CCC 628

6. What hope can you find in these verses?

Romans 6:5
2 Corinthians 4:10
Colossians 2:12

7. Explain these passages.

Romans 6:6
CCC 1696, 1697

8. Compare the following verses.

Romans 6:7
1 Peter 4:1

9. Find the hope and truth in Romans 6:8.

10. Use the catechism to define "justification." CCC 1987

11. How should you consider yourself? Romans 6:11

12. Why is it important for a soul to avoid sin? CCC 2819

13. Identify the warnings in these passages.

Romans 6:12–14
James 4:6–8
1 Peter 5:6–9

* What ways do you find helpful in resisting temptations to sin?

14. What can you learn from these verses?

Matthew 6:24
John 8:34–36
Romans 6:16

15. Where can you find freedom? John 8:31–32, 36

16. How can you become freer?

Romans 6:17
CCC 1733

17. Explain "sanctification."

Romans 6:19
CCC 1995

* Brainstorm some practical means of sanctification for yourself.

18. What is our end? Romans 6:21

19. What can you learn about death?

CCC 1006
CCC 1010

20. In your own words, explain the hope in Romans 6:23.

Conflict
Romans 7

Wretched man that I am!
Who will deliver me from this body of death?
Thanks be to God through Jesus Christ our Lord!
So then, I of myself serve the law of God with my mind,
but with my flesh I serve the law of sin.
Romans 7:24–25

Paul identifies the interior conflict between good and evil, between the law and sin. The Letter to the Romans contains very dense theology, and Romans Chapter 7 is a challenging chapter to unpack. Paul begins to make some analogies, but he leaves it to the reader to complete them. The overall goal is to consider the relationship between the law and grace. Why does the Christian, who has died with Christ and been filled with grace, continue to be tempted and to fall into sin? Why do believers fail to act like the saints that they have been empowered to become?

An analogy with marriage prepares one to consider the relationship between the Christian and the binding force of the prescriptions of the law in one's life. Married couples promise to love one another, for as long as they live. If one spouse breaks that marital vow, he or she is guilty of the mortal sin of adultery. But, when a spouse dies, the remaining spouse is released from the marital bond and is free to marry another. The marital covenant is binding only in this life.

Paul's first spouse was the old law, but his new spouse is Christ. The believer now belongs to Christ, the bridegroom. And Christ gives the gift of the Holy Spirit to help believers understand the truth concerning sin and resist temptation.

When Jesus during the discourse in the Upper Room foretells the coming of the Holy Spirit "at the price of" his own departure, and promises "I will send him to you," in the very same context he adds: "And when he comes, he will convince the world concerning sin and righteousness and judgment." The same Counselor and Spirit of truth who has been promised as the one who "will teach" and "bring to remembrance," who "will bear witness," and "guide into all the truth," in the words just quoted is foretold as the one who "will convince the world concerning sin and righteousness and judgment."
Pope (Saint) John Paul II, *Dominum et Vivificantem*, 18 May 1986, 27

Previously, the faithful were concerned with obeying the minute precepts of the law, in order to be pleasing to God. But now Jesus has come to fulfill and perfect the law. Jesus perfectly observes all of the precepts of the law, and He gives a more demanding law to His followers—the law of love. *"This is my commandment, that you love one another as I have loved you. Greater love has no man than this, that a man lay down his life for his friends"* (John 15:12–13). Jesus did not come to abolish the law but to fulfill it. The way in which a Christian fulfills the law requires the power of the Holy Spirit and grace.

Paul defends the law. Where would the world be without the Mosaic Law? God knew that human beings would need direction and boundaries. But, the law, in itself, cannot provide the grace to be obedient to God.

So what does the Law from which we are liberated and which does not save mean? For Saint Paul, as for all his contemporaries, the word "Law" meant the Torah in its totality, that is, the five books of Moses. The Torah, in the Pharisaic interpretation, that which Paul had studied and made his own, was a complex set of conduct codes that ranged from the ethical nucleus to observances of rites and worship and that essentially determined the identity of the just person. In particular, these included circumcision, observances concerning pure food and ritual purity in general, the rules regarding the observance of the Sabbath, etc. codes of conduct that also appear frequently in the debates between Jesus and his contemporaries.

. . . Paul, who had learned these observances in their role of defending God's gift, of the inheritance of faith in one God alone, saw this identity threatened by the freedom of the Christians; this is why he persecuted them. At the moment of his encounter with the Risen One, he understood that with Christ's Resurrection the situation had changed radically. With Christ, the God of Israel, the one true God became the God of all peoples. . . . Paul knows that in the twofold love of God and neighbor the whole of the Law is present and carried out. Thus in communion with Christ, in a faith that creates charity, the entire Law is fulfilled. We become just by entering into communion with Christ who is Love.

Pope Benedict XVI, General Audience, 19 November 2008

Despite the goodness of the law, sin continues to reign. Paul uses personification to represent the abstract concept of inanimate sin as if it were a person. Sometimes it seems as if Paul is using the term "sin" as synonymous with temptation or concupiscence—the human appetite for disordered desires, which humanity inherited as a curse from the fall of Adam and Eve. Paul's consideration of the commandments elucidates the ways in which he has fallen short. However, the law lacks the power to bring life. Without the law, how would one know right from wrong, or what is pleasing or displeasing to God? Hence, ultimately the law provides a service to humanity. *So the law is holy, and the commandment is holy and just and good* (Romans 7:12). The law is good; commandments are good. Sin is bad. The law cannot fix the sin problem. Sinners need grace.

Describing the interior conflict between good and evil—Paul seems to identify the lack of consistency between creed, cult, and conduct. Orthodoxy is right belief and sound doctrine. Orthopraxy is right behavior. The Christian strives to match behavior to belief. But the believer often falls short. *I do not understand my own actions. For I do not do what I want, but I do the very thing I hate* (Romans 7:15). Paul is not alone in observing and identifying this problem.

> "I like your Christ,
> I do not like your Christians.
> Your Christians do not act like your Christ."
>
> Mahatma Ghandi

Paul identifies a problem that is familiar to all of us. Why do Christians sometimes behave so badly? Why are some pagans kind and generous? Why do the same sins plague us, again and again, even after we have confessed them and resolved to amend our lives? The fictional Anne Shirley, in *Anne of Green Gables,* said, "Being good comes naturally to some people, but that has never been the case for me." We want to be healthy, but cannot seem to do what the doctor prescribes. We want to be thin and fit, but we will not exercise and eat properly. We want to speak kindly of others, but gossip seems to roll off the tongue.

Most people want to be good. Students want to excel in school. They want to make good grades, but they go out to play rather than study. Children want to grow up to be great athletes or musicians, but they refuse to practice. Couples want to have an excellent marriage and family life, but they fail to make the investment necessary to create a loving marriage and strong family life. People want to be decent neighbors and noble citizens, but it takes so much time and effort. Folks want to make friends, but it is so much easier to just isolate oneself and stay home. Virtue takes effort and grace. Many want to become saints, but sinning seems to be the default.

> Never does anyone enjoy health by his willing it, nor is he freed from illness and disease because he chooses and desires it. What good is it to desire the grace of health unless God, who grants the very use of life, imparts also the vigor of its preservation? That it might be more evidently clear that even through natural goodness, which is bestowed by the munificence of the Creator, sometimes the first beginnings of a good will arise, which, however, unless they be directed by God, cannot achieve the full performance of virtues, the Apostle is witness, when he says: "Now, to will belongs to me; but I do not find the means to accomplish what is good" (Romans 7:18).
> Saint John Cassian (AD 360–435), *Conferences, 2, 13, 9*

Perhaps the problem results from failure to identify what must be done to achieve the goal. A seminary rector confided that some seminarians longed to be great evangelists, but could not find the time to pray. They all desired to be great preachers, but they did not want to study. The rector knew that prayer releases the power of God for evangelism, and great preachers study hard. So the believer needs knowledge of the good, the grace to do it, and then the will to act.

> "Pray as though everything depends on God.
> Work as though everything depends on you."
> Saint Augustine

The problem that all human beings face is the sin problem. We know right from wrong in our hearts, but we lack the grace and willpower to behave as we ought. Even those who know the commandments struggle to be obedient. While sin is enticing, promising thrills and enjoyment, soon the wages of sin become apparent—suffering in this life and eternal death in the world to come. However, the righteous God provides a solution to the sin problem. He sends His only Son to die for the sins of the world. Then the Holy Spirit comes to provide grace for the believer to live in ways pleasing to God. *Who will deliver me from the body of death? Thanks be to God through Jesus Christ our Lord!* (Romans 7:24–25).

Donald Calloway was not raised in a church-going family. His teen-aged mother was married several times, finally to a military man. In excessive teen-age rebellion, Donald broke most of the commandments—lying, stealing, using drugs, disobeying his parents and authorities, cursing, committing violent acts, and indulging in sexual promiscuity. Ultimately, he was arrested and spent time in drug rehabilitation facilities. Nothing seemed to help him, until his mother became a Catholic and started praying the rosary for him.

One night, out of boredom, Donald picked up a book about Marian apparitions that transformed his life. He went to a daily Mass the following morning but understood almost nothing of the liturgy. He couldn't understand how the people all stood together and then knelt at exactly the same time! He looked for strings above their heads, like marionettes. Donald asked to see a priest. He trashed his drug paraphernalia, began praying the rosary, and studied the Catholic faith.

Donald tasted the amazing mercy of God and experienced the transforming power of God's grace. He became a Catholic, and today, Father Donald Calloway is a priest of the Congregation of Marian Fathers of the Immaculate Conception of the Most Blessed Virgin Mary, preaching about the Divine Mercy of God, at the National Shrine of Divine Mercy in Stockbridge, Massachusetts.

1. Compare the following verses.

Romans 7:1
Galatians 2:19
Colossians 1:21–22

2. Explain the law concerning marriage. Romans 7:2–3

3. Christ was raised from the dead so that believers may do what?

Romans 7:4b
Galatians 5:22–23

* Which gift of the Holy Spirit is most evident in your life? Which do you need?

4. How does sin come about?

Romans 7:5
James 1:15

5. Under what do Christians now serve? Romans 7:6b

6. What does the law accomplish? Is it good or bad? Romans 7:7–8

7. What does the Catechism reveal about the law? CCC 2542

8. Why should people keep the law? Leviticus 18:5

9. Ultimately, what does Paul conclude about the Law? Romans 7:12

10. According to Christian tradition, show some functions of the law. CCC 1963

Like a tutor, it . . .
denounces and discloses . . .
prepares and disposes . . .

11. What does Paul say about sin? Romans 7:13–14

* Find some evidence of the sin problem in the world today.

12. Explain three conditions determining mortal sin. CCC 1857

CCC 1858
CCC 1859
CCC 1859

13. What can diminish culpability for sin? CCC 1860

14. Explain Paul's dilemma in Romans 7:15.

* Can you share a time when you experienced the same dilemma as Paul?

15. Explain the battle between flesh and spirit.

Romans 7:18–19
1 Corinthians 3:1
Galatians 5:17

** List some ways to walk in the spirit, rather than the flesh.

16. Use a dictionary to define "justification." CCC 1994

17. How can you approach the law?

Psalm 1:1–2
Psalm 119:97
Romans 7:22

18. What is the source of your justification? CCC 1996

19. Who effects your sanctification? CCC 1995

20. Who can deliver us from sin? Romans 7:25

* Brainstorm some practical means of attaining sanctifying grace.

CHAPTER 8

Life in the Spirit
Romans 8

If the Spirit of him who raised Jesus from the dead dwells in you,
he who raised Christ Jesus from the dead
will give life to your mortal bodies also
through his Spirit who dwells in you.
Romans 8:11

Life in the Spirit—the heart of the Letter to the Romans can be found in Romans 8. After showing the perfect righteousness of God contrasted against the sinfulness of humanity, Paul now gives a message of hope to sinners. *There is therefore now no condemnation for those who are in Christ Jesus* (Romans 8:1). God does for humanity what the law could not do. Jesus frees the repentant sinner from the consequences of sin and sends the indwelling of the Holy Sprit. When a person has faith and is baptized, he receives the power to resist the sins of the flesh.

In the Incarnation, Jesus came to pay the price for the sins of humanity. *And the Word became flesh and dwelt among us, full of grace and truth* (John 1:14). *And being found in human form he humbled himself and became obedient unto death, even death on a cross* (Philippians 2:8). Those who are in Christ Jesus are justified and brought into right relationship with God the Father, by His death.

Thus, we can see clearly that even before he does anything, the Christian already possesses a rich and fruitful interiority, given to him in the Sacraments of Baptism and Confirmation, an interiority which establishes him in an objective and original relationship of sonship with God. This is our greatest dignity: to be not merely images but also children of God. And it is an invitation to live our sonship, to be increasingly aware that we are adoptive sons in God's great family. It is an invitation to transform this objective gift into a subjective reality, decisive for our way of thinking, acting and being.
Pope Benedict XVI, *General Audience, 15 November 2006*

The battle between the sinful flesh and the Spirit of God continues until death. But now the Christian has the means with which to resist sin, which the law could not provide. The believer no longer has a spirit of slavery to sin; now the Spirit of God enables believers to become adopted sons of God the Father. Adoption in the ancient world enabled an individual to become part of a noble family and enjoy blessings and privileges that were new and beyond him. Christians receive adoption into the family of God with divine favors that are enjoyed by Jesus the Son. They become heirs and partakers in His Father's glory.

> For Saint Paul teaches, *all who are led by the Spirit of God are children of God*. The filiation of divine adoption is born in man on the basis of the mystery of the Incarnation, therefore through Christ the eternal Son. But the birth, or rebirth, happens when God the Father *sends the Spirit of his Son into our hearts*. Then *we receive a spirit of adopted sons by which we cry "Abba, Father!"* Hence the divine filiation planted in the human soul through sanctifying grace is the work of the Holy Spirit. *It is the Spirit himself bearing witness with our spirit that we are children of God, and if children, then heirs, heirs of God and fellow heirs with Christ*. Sanctifying grace is the principle and source of man's new life: divine, supernatural life.
>
> Saint Pope John Paul II, *Dominum et Vivificantem*, 18 May 1996, 52

The term "Abba" is an Aramaic term. Jesus uttered this during His passion: *"Abba, Father, all things are possible to you, remove this chalice from me; yet not what I will, but what you will"* (Mark 14:36). Even to this day in the Holy Land, one can hear children and adults using this endearing term of intimacy with their natural, biological fathers. The Holy Spirit grants a special privilege to Christians in allowing this familiarity with the Creator of the universe.

Christians are children of God and fellow heirs with Christ, *provided we suffer with him in order that we may also be glorified with him* (Romans 8:17). Some preachers promote a "prosperity gospel"—"just believe in Jesus and your life will be bliss." Catholic theology, in contrast, advances the full gospel, in which suffering in this life will always exist. Believing in Jesus doesn't ensure that all trouble will vanish. Rather, God gives the Christian all the grace necessary to conquer sin and embrace suffering. Redemptive suffering enables one to unite his or her suffering with that of Christ in love. Believers offer up suffering to God for some good purpose. We accept sufferings with Christ in order to be glorified with Him in the end.

The glory to be revealed—Christians hope to stay faithful to Christ during their earthly lives so that they might be united with Him in the world to come. *I consider that the sufferings of this present time are not worth comparing with the glory that is to be revealed to us* (Romans 8:18). Elsewhere, Saint Paul writes: *"What no eye has seen, nor ear heard, nor the heart of man conceived, what God has prepared for those who love him," God has revealed to us through the Spirit* (1 Corinthians 2:9–10). Christians are strangers and sojourners in this world, awaiting a new heaven and a new earth and the heavenly Jerusalem. It is in this hope that sinners are saved. And it is necessary for believers to hope without seeing, and for them to wait in patience for the fulfillment of all God's promises.

We know that in everything God works for good with those who love him, who are called according to his purpose (Romans 8:28). This passage indicates that God will use our sufferings and our struggles for some good end. It would be wrong to assume that everything works for good <u>in this life</u>. Paul doesn't say that. We know that God will work all things for good *in His time,* not ours. But some people read this verse to expect that everything will work out according to their plans and dreams right now. The glory that Christians hope to experience will come later.

What will be that glory, and how great the joy of being admitted to the sight of God! to be so honored as to receive the joy of eternal light and salvation in the presence of Christ the Lord, your God! to greet Abraham, and Isaac, and Jacob, and all the patriarchs, apostles, prophets, and martyrs! to rejoice with the just and with the friends of God in the kingdom of heaven, in the delight of the immortality that will be given! to receive there what eye has not seen nor ear heard, what has not entered into the heart of man!

The Apostle predicts that we will receive even greater things than we perform or suffer here, when he says: *The sufferings of the present time are not worth comparing with the brightness about to come upon us and which will be unveiled in us.* When that unveiling has come and when the brightness of God shines about us, honored by the condescension of the Lord, we shall be as blessed and joyful as they will remain guilty and miserable.

Saint Cyprian of Carthage (†AD 258),
Letter of Cyprian to the People of Thibar, 58, 56, 10

God reveals a schematic plan of salvation. *For those whom he foreknew he also predestined to be conformed to the image of his Son, in order that he might be the first-born among many brethren* (Romans 8:29). God knows each and every person whom He creates. *"Before I formed you in the womb I knew you, and before you were born I created you"* (Jeremiah 1:5). God calls and invites each person to repent and accept His mercy. Those who respond to God's call are justified by His grace for righteousness. And those who are justified will be glorified with Him, after they have repented of sin, endured suffering, and run the race to the finish.

Whoever says that God does not will all men to be saved, but only the certain number of the predestined, is saying a harsher thing than ought to be said of the inscrutable depth of the grace of God, who both wills that all should be saved and come to a knowledge of the truth, and fulfills the proposal of His will in those whom, when He foreknew them, He predestined, when He predestined them, He called, when He called them, He justified, and, when He justified them, He glorified.
. . . And thus, those who are saved are saved because God willed them to be saved, and those who perish do perish because they deserved to perish.

Saint Prosper of Aquitaine (†AD 455),
*Responses on behalf of Augustine to the Articles of Objections
Raised by his Calumniators in Gaul, 8*

Predestination involves the act of divine intelligence and foreknowledge. Although this is a mystery, Catholic teaching holds that predestination does not negate free will. God is omniscient and knows all things, even before they happen. And yet God wills all men to be saved and gives grace to all, knowing that some will reject it.

God is on our side. *If God is for us, who is against us? He who did not spare his own Son but gave him up for us all, will he not also give us all things with him* (Romans 8:31b–32)? God has given everything to humanity. He has given each person an eternal soul, life, grace, and the hope of eternal glory with Him in heaven. *For God so loved the world that he gave his only begotten Son, that whoever believes in him should not perish but have eternal life. For God did not send his Son into the world to condemn the world, but that the world might be saved through him* (John 3:16–17). God's gift in sending Jesus to pay the ultimate price to save sinful humanity proves that God is on our side. He wants to save each person.

What can separate the believer from the love of Christ and eternal salvation? Only SIN can separate anyone from God's love. Tribulation, distress, persecution, famine, nakedness, peril, and sword are all manifestations of suffering, but none of the above involves sin. Saint Paul experienced most of those adversities during his missionary journeys. *Three times I have been beaten with rods; once I was stoned. Three times I have been shipwrecked* (2 Corinthians 11:25). Paul continued to cling to Jesus in the midst of his sufferings and distress.

In all adversity and distress, Christians can be more than conquerors, with God's grace and assistance. The poetic closing of this chapter gives great hope and confidence to believers. *For I am sure that neither death, nor life, nor angels, nor principalities, nor things present, nor things to come, nor powers, nor height, nor depth, nor anything else in all creation, will be able to separate us from the love of God in Christ Jesus our Lord* (Romans 8:38–39). Nothing in the world is greater than God, and nothing can surpass God's love and protection.

An only child growing up with atheist parents, Jennifer refused to pray the sinner's prayer at a Christian summer camp and left a secular Texas college, even though her parents and grandparents were alumni, because it was "too Christian." She mocked her soon-to-be-husband when he shared how he felt as he was being baptized as a young adult. Jennifer made good money in the high tech industry and married a great guy with graduate degrees in business and law. She should have been blissfully happy, but darkness settled over her. As an atheist, she wondered if anything really mattered. Her book, *Something Other Than God—How I Passionately Sought Happiness and Accidentally Found It*, relates her quest to find truth and meaning, and her surprising journey into the Catholic Church. Today, Jennifer and Joe Fulwiler and their six children live in Austin, Texas, and Jennifer hosts a daily program on Catholic radio: The Jennifer Fulwiler Show. God loved and sought out Jennifer, even when she wasn't looking for Him.

1. Explain the hope and confidence in Romans 8:1.

2. What new law characterizes the people of God?

Romans 8:2–3
CCC 602

3. On what should you set your mind? Romans 8:5–8

4. List some titles of the Holy Spirit. Romans 8:9, CCC 693

5. What hope can you find in these passages?

John 5:21
Romans 8:11
CCC 632
CCC 658
CCC 989
CCC 990

6. Identify evidence of the Holy Spirit. Romans 8:10, Galatians 5:22–23

7. What relationship is imparted to Christians, with what privilege?

Romans 8:14	
Romans 8:15	
Romans 8:16	
Romans 8:17	

* How do you relate to and pray to God as your Father?

8. What did Jesus ask? What does beatitude do for us?

John 17:3–5	
Romans 8:18	
CCC 1721	

** How do you imagine the glory of heaven?

9. What is the destiny of the cosmos?

Romans 8:19–23
Revelation 21:1–2
CCC 1046

10. In what virtue were you saved? Define it.

Romans 8:24–25
Hebrews 11:1
CCC 1817
CCC 1818–1819

* How is this virtue manifest in your personal life?

11. Who and what helps in our weakness?

Romans 8:26–27
CCC 741
CCC 2559

12. In your own words explain Romans 8:28. What does it NOT mean?

13. How long has God known you?

Psalm 139:1–13
Jeremiah 1:5
Romans 8:29

14. What can you learn about predestination?

Romans 8:29
1 Peter 1:20
CCC 257
CCC 600
CCC 2782

* When have you felt God calling you?

15. What two things does God do for those He calls? Romans 8:30b

16. What confidence can you find in these verses?

Psalm 118:6
Romans 8:31
Romans 8:32

17. Who is the contender, the adversary?

Isaiah 50:8–9
Romans 8:33
CCC 2852

18. Who intercedes for believers? Romans 8:27, 34

19. What can and cannot separate us from the love of Christ?

Sirach 10:13
Romans 8:35
Ephesians 2:12

20. How can we be more than conquerors? Romans 8:37

Monthly Social Activity

This month, your small group will meet for coffee, tea, or a simple breakfast, lunch, or dessert in someone's home. Pray for this social event and for the host or hostess. Try, if at all possible, to attend.

Think about a time in which God enabled you to see or hear about something miraculous—a healing, a financial burden lifted, a new baby, or a better job.

Some examples:

✤ *My friend was going blind and receiving injections in her eye. We went to a healing Mass in our parish. When she told the priest her problem, he prayed over her. God healed her and she was free from problems for five years.*

✤ *A childless couple were praying for a baby, when friends at church took in a pregnant teen relative from out-of-state. When the teen met the couple, she chose them to be the adoptive parents of her child.*

✤ *A neighbor invited a couple on the verge of divorce to go to a course at church that would save their marriage. The couple showed up at a "Life In the Spirit Seminar," where God delivered the husband of alcoholism and drug addiction.*

CHAPTER 9

Israel, God's Elect
Romans 9

They are Israelites,
and to them belong the sonship, the glory,
the covenants, the giving of the law,
the worship, and the promises;
to them belong the patriarchs,
and of their race, according to the flesh, is the Christ,
who is God over all, blessed for ever.
Amen.
Romans 9:4–5

Israel, God's Chosen People—*"I have made a covenant with my chosen one, I have sworn to David my servant: 'I will establish your descendants for ever, and build your throne for all generations'"* (Psalm 89:3). God has made promises to Abraham and to his descendants, the Chosen People. *For the LORD has chosen Zion; he has desired it for his habitation: "This is my resting place for ever; here I will dwell, for I have desired it. I will abundantly bless her provisions; I will satisfy her poor with bread. Her priests I will clothe with salvation, and her saints will shout for joy"* (Psalm 132:13–15). Will God continue to be faithful to His promises to Israel? Is God righteous? Does God abandon the Jewish people?

Remember that Jesus, Mary, and Joseph are Jews. Peter and all of the apostles are Jews. Paul has been preaching the gospel to Jews and Gentiles, but more Gentiles seem to be responding to God's grace and accepting the gift of baptism. Because of Paul's success in evangelizing the pagans, it may seem as if Paul no longer cares about God's Chosen People. The larger question relates to God's faithfulness to the covenant He made with Israel. Does God's election of Israel still hold true?

Paul expresses profound sorrow that his Jewish kinsmen are not responding to the grace and invitation to follow Christ. *I am speaking the truth in Christ, I am not lying: my conscience bears me witness in the Holy Spirit, that I have great sorrow and unceasing anguish in my heart. For I could wish that I myself were accursed and cut off from Christ for the sake of my brethren, my kinsmen according to the flesh* (Romans 9:1–3). Wait a minute! Would Paul forsake his relationship with Christ for the sake of the Jews? How could that be? Here again, Paul uses the literary device of exaggeration to make a point. Paul is not literally suggesting that he would relinquish his salvation for the redemption of others. Indeed, Paul will be martyred for his faith in Jesus, in AD 64 in Rome. Rather, Paul expresses the great love that he has for his kinsmen in wanting to do anything possible, even go to great extremes, to aid their cause and inspire them to accept salvation in Christ. The Messiah has come, but many cannot or will not accept Him.

Salvation comes from the Jews, not from the Jewish law, but from the Jewish Messiah—Jesus Christ, Our Lord. The promise to David comes to fruition in Jesus, the descendant of David and Son of God. What greater privilege could any nation or people enjoy? *They are Israelites, and to them belong the sonship, the glory, the covenants, the giving of the law, the worship, and the promises; to them belong the patriarchs, and of their race, according to the flesh, is the Christ, who is God over all, blessed for ever. Amen* (Romans 9:4–5). Paul recounts the many ways in which God has blessed His Chosen People. God has not failed to honor His promises.

Not all Israelites are children of the promise. Being in the Jewish bloodline does not guarantee that one is a true Israelite. There are faithful, observant, God-fearing Jews, and there are others who care nothing for God. The same could be said of Christians. Just because one's name is O'Brien or Wolski does not ensure that he or she is a good Irish Catholic or a devout Polish Catholic. The Lord's choice of Israel shows His divine prerogative, irrespective of any human merit. God's ways are not our ways. Sometimes God turns things upside down. The younger serves the older, the weak becomes strong, and the mighty are cast down. God's purpose of election indicates His call. *"Yet I have loved Jacob but I have hated Esau"* (Malachi 1:2) does not reflect human emotions, but rather God's call. Elsewhere in the Bible, God shows a concern for Esau's descendants—the Edomites—as well. *"You shall not abhor an Edomite, for he is your brother"* (Deuteronomy 23:7).

Is God fair or unfair? *"I will have mercy on whom I have mercy, and I will have compassion on whom I have compassion"* (Romans 9:15). The psalmist trusts in God's love: *Great is your mercy, O LORD; give me life according to your justice* (Psalm 119:156). God's mercy, beyond human comprehension, exists alongside God's perfect justice, which also transcends human understanding. The perfect mercy of God and the perfect justice of God are divine mysteries.

> *It is a question not of him who wills nor of him who runs, but of God's showing mercy.* . . . There are some people who are so proud of their successes that they attribute everything to themselves and nothing to Him who made them and gave them wisdom and supplied them with good things. Let them learn of this saying that even to wish someone well requires God's help, or rather, that even to choose what is right is something divine and a gift of God's benevolence to man. *Not of him who wills;* that is, *not only* of him who wills; and not *only* of him who runs, but *also* of God's showing mercy. Since to will is also from God, it is reasonable that Paul attributed the whole to God. However well you may run, however well you may wrestle, you still need Him who gives the crown.
>
> Saint Gregory Nazianzen (AD 330–389),
> *On the Words of the Gospel in Matthew, 37, 13*

Why did God harden Pharaoh's heart? Recall the ten plagues in Exodus. Moses repeatedly asked Pharaoh to let God's people go into the wilderness to offer sacrifice, and Pharaoh continually refused. God sent plagues to show His power to Pharaoh, and still Pharaoh refused to accede to God's demands. Only after sending many requests and plagues did God punish Pharaoh. God gave Pharaoh many opportunities and second chances before He ultimately confirmed what Pharaoh had chosen. Pharaoh had hardened his heart against God, and God confirmed that choice. God honors free will. After a time, God allows us to have our way.

> God created us with free will, and we are not forced by necessity either to virtue or to vice. Otherwise, where there were necessity there would be no crown. Just as with good works, it is God who brings them to perfection, depending not so much on him that wills nor on him that runs as on God who pities and assists him to reach the goal; so too with wickedness and sin, the seed that prompts us is our own, while its germination and maturation belongs to the devil.
>
> Saint Jerome (AD 347–420), *Against Jovinian, 2, 3*

God has made all people to know the riches of His glory. Recall the story from the Prophet Isaiah: *Shall the potter be regarded as the clay; that the thing made should say of its maker, "He did not make me"; or the thing formed say "He has no understanding"* (Isaiah 29:16)? God has fashioned each person in a unique and individual way; in a similar way the potter fashions different clay pots for different uses. And yet no potter molds a vessel with the intent of throwing it away. God wants each person to become the perfect person He has created him to be.

Paul recalls the prophet Hosea, who was married to an unfaithful wife, just as God is joined to Israel, who proves to be unfaithful, time and again. *"Those who were not my people I will call 'my people,' and her who was not beloved I will call 'my beloved'"* (Hosea 2:23; Romans 9:25). God reaches beyond His Chosen People to love those people outside the covenant, inviting them into relationship with Him as well. God will save a remnant of the sons of Israel, and then He will go beyond. Moreover, God has prepared children, not only from the Jews, but also from the Gentiles, beforehand for His glory (Romans 9:23–24).

> "O Blessed light, O Trinity and first Unity!" God is eternal blessedness, undying life, unfading light. God is love: Father, Son, and Holy Spirit. God freely wills to communicate the glory of his blessed life. Such is the "plan of his loving kindness," conceived by the Father before the foundation of the world, in his beloved Son: "He destined us in love to be his sons" and "to be conformed to the image of his Son," through "the spirit of sonship." This plan is a "grace [which] was given to us in Christ Jesus before the ages began," stemming immediately from Trinitarian love. It unfolds in the work of creation, the whole history of salvation after the fall, and the missions of the Son and the Spirit, which are continued in the mission of the Church.   CCC 257

Predestination is an unfathomable mystery of God. In the widest sense, it reflects every eternal decision of God; and, in a narrow sense, predestination involves the supernatural final destiny of all souls. God's eternal decision assumes certain souls into heaven's eternal glory with Him. Catholic teaching holds that predestination by God does not deny human free will. And although the omniscient God *knows* beforehand that some souls will reject His mercy, God does not *will* that anyone be lost. Complete predestination involves the divine preparation of grace in this present, earthly life, and of eternal bliss and glory in the world to come.

> It was not because we did believe, but so that we might believe, that He chose us, so that we could be said to have chosen him first, and perish the thought, the Scriptural saying be false: *"You did not choose Me, but I chose you"* (John 15:16). We are called, not because we believed, but so that we might believe; and by that calling which is without repentance it is effected and carried through that we should believe.
>
> Saint Augustine of Hippo (AD 354–430),
> *The Predestination of the Saints, 19, 38*

Jesus Christ is a stumbling block for some. God calls on the human heart, but some will not respond. In Paul's time, many people were looking for a military leader to restore Israel's prior political dominance. Even today, people reject the Prince of Peace. Some people are looking for peace, love, and joy in situations and structures that can never satisfy them. Nevertheless, God continues to send His grace to people to enable them to believe in Jesus Christ, his Son.

Roy Schoemann, on observant Jew, expected to have a personal encounter with God at his Bar Mitzvah. He expected the veil to be lifted, but he was disappointed. Continuing his studies in Judaism, Roy was mentored by a prominent rabbi and visited Israel. He excelled in college and became a professor at Harvard. However, while in college, Roy lost his faith and plunged into an existentialist angst. While walking on the beach in Massachusetts one day, Roy was enveloped in Love. He saw his whole life unfold before him. Roy experienced the presence of God and prayed that he would come to know His Name. "If you are Buddha, I will become a Buddhist, if Krishna, I will be Hari Krishna, but don't even think . . ."

One year to the date from that prayer, Roy had an encounter with the Blessed Virgin Mother, the most beautiful woman he had ever seen. She conversed with him, and Roy realized that Mary's Son Jesus Christ is Israel's Messiah. Nonetheless, it would take another decade before Roy would be baptized and enter into the Catholic Church. He is the author of *Salvation is from the Jews* and *Honey from the Rock,* and he remains a popular Hebrew Catholic speaker and evangelist.

1. How strongly does Paul feel about his kinsmen? Romans 9:1–3

2. Who else had a similar sentiment? Exodus 32:31–32

3. What privileges have the Jews been given? Romans 9:4–5

4. What link do Catholics have with the Jewish people? CCC 839

5. How does God love Israel?

CCC 219
CCC 220

6. Does God's Word fail?

Romans 9:6
1 Peter 1:24–25

* List some promises that God has made to you.

7. Who are the children of God? Romans 9:8–9

8. Explain God's purpose of election. Romans 9:10–13

9. What can you learn about God's mercy?

Exodus 33:19
Psalm 51:1
Psalm 103:1–4
Sirach 5:6

* Describe a situation in which you showed mercy to someone.

10. Compare the following verses.

Isaiah 29:16
Isaiah 45:9
Romans 9:19–24

** For what purpose do you think God formed you? Any special task or work?

11. To whom does Hosea's prophecy refer?

Hosea 2:23
Romans 9:25–26
1 Peter 2:10

12. Recall God's promise to Abraham. Genesis 22:17–18

13. What did Isaiah prophecy concerning this promise? Isaiah 10:21–23

14. What happened at Sodom and Gomorrah and why? Genesis 18:16–19:29

15. Who survived? Genesis 19:15–23

— Who did not survive? Genesis 19:26

* What danger or merit is there in looking back on your life and choices?

16. What is necessary to attain righteousness? Romans 9:30

Romans 3:22–24
Galatians 2:16
Philippians 3:9

* How can you strengthen your faith in Jesus?

17. Why do some people fail to attain righteousness? Romans 9:32

18. What are works of the law? CCC 578–579

19. Contrast "works of the law" with "works of mercy." CCC 2447

** Identify a work of mercy that you can do this week, and then do it!

20. Who is the stone that makes some stumble? Romans 9:33, 1 Peter 2:4ff

CHAPTER 10

Believers in Christ
Romans 10

For there is no distinction between Jew and Greek;
the same Lord is Lord of all and bestows his riches upon all who call upon him.
For "every one who calls upon the name of the Lord will be saved."
Romans 10:12–13

God desires salvation for all. Because Paul's preaching to the Gentiles had proven so successful, with so many people hearing the Gospel and believing in Jesus, Paul must have been challenged about his loyalty to his own people—the Jews. In the previous chapter, Paul expressed great sorrow and anguish of heart for his people. Now he reveals his sincere hope for the Jews: *Brethren, my heart's desire and prayer to God for them is that they may be saved* (Romans 10:1). Paul clearly loves his kinsmen, but he becomes frustrated at their reluctance to accept of the Gospel.

Zeal for the Mosaic Law, while good, remains inadequate for bridging the gap between sinful humanity and the perfect, righteous God. Only Jesus perfectly obeyed all the precepts of the Law. Jesus highlights the difference between God's Law and human interpretation of the precepts. He accused the Pharisees of demanding strict observance to minute details of the law, while neglecting the weightier demands for trust, integrity, and love. *"Woe to you, scribes and Pharisees, hypocrites! for you tithe mint and dill and cumin, and have neglected the weightier matters of the law, justice and mercy and faith; these you ought to have done, without neglecting the others"* (Matthew 23:23). Faith, hope, and love preempt all the other laws. Both Jews and Christians can become trapped by focusing on minutiae, while neglecting love for God and neighbor.

Jesus manifested His power in miracles, signs, and wonders that everyone could see and hear about from eyewitnesses. *For Christ is the end of the law, that every one who has faith may be justified* (Romans 10:4). Jesus is the visible perfection of the Law and the fulfillment of the prophecies of old.

Christ is the end that perfects, not the end that destroys. For that is called the end for the sake of which everything is done that is done in reference to something else . . . Just as the knowledge that we now have will be *put away*, as the Apostle says, when we have that knowledge which he calls *face to face*, so too it is necessary that the things given in shadows to the Jews in the Old Testament be put away by the revelation of the New Testament.

Saint Augustine of Hippo (AD 354–430),
Against an Adversary of the Law and the Prophets, 2, 7, 26

Jesus manifests righteousness based on faith. He worked miracles; then the most amazing event in all of human history occurred when Jesus Christ arose from the dead and appeared alive to His friends and followers. Faith requires the acceptance of the word of another and an adherence to the truth. How could the people of Paul's time have ignored the revelation of God in Jesus? How could people of ANY time in history reject the mercy and love of God in the Risen Christ?

> The believer has sufficient motive for believing, for he is moved by the authority of Divine teaching confirmed by miracles, and what is more, by the inward instinct of the Divine invitation: hence he does not believe lightly.
>
> Grace causes faith not only when faith begins anew to be in a man, but also as long as faith lasts. For . . . God is always working man's justification, even as the sun is always lighting up the air. Hence grace is not less effective when it comes to a believer than when it comes to an unbeliever: since it causes faith in both, in the former by confirming and perfecting it, in the latter by creating it anew. . . . Grace does not cause faith in one who has it already: just as, on the other hand, a second mortal sin does not take away grace from one who has already lost it [*grace*] through a previous mortal sin.
>
> Saint Thomas Aquinas (AD 1225–1274),
> *The Summa Theologica, II, II, Q2, 9. Q4, 3*

Moses told the people that God's word would be in their hearts. *"For this commandment which I command you this day is not too hard for you, neither is it far off. It is not in heaven, that you should say 'Who will go up for us to heaven, and bring it to us, that we may hear it and do it?' Neither is it beyond the sea, that you should say, 'Who will go over the sea for us, and bring it to us, that we may hear it and do it?' But the word is very near you; it is in your mouth and in your heart, so that you can do it. See, I have set before you this day life and good, death and evil"* (Deuteronomy 30:11–15). Jesus came down from heaven to bring salvation to the world, then descended into the abyss and arose from the dead. The Resurrection of Jesus proves that God has sent a Savior to conquer sin and death and offer eternal life to those who believe. *"Who will ascend into heaven?"* (Romans 10:7). Jesus came from heaven and returned (Mark 16:19, Acts 1:9–11).

Believe, confess, and be saved. Paul encourages people to put their faith in Jesus, accept salvation, and be justified before God the Father. Catholics profess this faith in the sacraments of Baptism and Confirmation, and they proclaim this profession of faith in the Nicene Creed at every Sunday Mass. *If you confess with your lips that Jesus is Lord and believe in your heart that God raised him from the dead, you will be saved. For man believes with his heart and so is justified, and he confesses with his lips and so is saved. . . . For, "every one who calls upon the name of the Lord will be saved"* (Romans 10:9–10, 13). Here Paul recalls the prophecy of Joel (Joel 2:28–32), and the sermon of Saint Peter on Pentecost (Acts 2:17–21).

BELIEF ➤ CONFESSION ➤ SALVATION ➤ JUSTIFICATION

Confess with your lips—JESUS IS LORD!

Believe in your heart—GOD raised JESUS from the dead.

Call upon the Name of the Lord—Be saved.

Paul insists that there is no distinction between the Chosen People and non-Jews. Rather, God loves all people and showers blessings upon people of every land and nation. *For there is no distinction between Jew and Greek; the same Lord is Lord of all and bestows his riches upon all who call upon him* (Romans 10:12). God wants everyone to believe and be saved, Gentiles as well as Jews. Therefore, there is no good reason for anyone to remain in sin and separation from God. Everything has been provided by Jesus to deliver sinful humanity from shame.

Evangelize—Preach the Good News! Here Paul gives a conundrum. *But how are men to call upon him in whom they have not believed? And how are they to believe in him of whom they have never heard? And how are they to hear without a preacher? And how can men preach unless they are sent? As it is written, "How beautiful are the feet of those who preach good news"* (Romans 10:14–15).

How can you call upon a Redeemer—without faith?
How can you have faith in a Savior—of whom you have never heard?
How can you learn about Jesus—without an evangelist?
How can an evangelist preach—without being anointed and commissioned?
The Good News is heard—by the preaching of Christ.

Before ascending into heaven, Jesus commissioned the disciples. *"Go therefore and make disciples of all nations, baptizing them in the name of the Father and of the Son and of the Holy Spirit, teaching them to observe all that I have commanded you; and behold, I am with you always, to the close of the age"* (Matthew 18:19–20). This Great Commission, embraced first by Jesus' apostles, continues to this day. The words and works of Jesus continue to spread out to all the earth, and today there are more than 2.4 billion Christians in the world.

The Resurrection of Jesus Christ from the dead remains the single most amazing, spectacular event in all of human history. Paul encountered Jesus on the road to Damascus and spent the rest of his life telling others about Jesus. Meeting Jesus— believing in Him, growing closer to Him, and loving and praising Him—is the most important thing that can happen in any person's life, and sharing Jesus with others brings immense joy and eternal reward. Without grace, one cannot come to faith. And so Christians pray for the grace of salvation for lost souls and seek opportunities to share the Good News with others, whenever possible.

For by grace, [Paul] says, *you have been saved*. But lest the greatness of the benefits inflate you, see how he brings you down: *By grace you have been saved*, he says, *through faith*. And then again, lest a violence be done free will, after he has added what pertains to us he takes it away again when he says, *and that not of ourselves*. The faith, he means, is not from ourselves; for if He had not come, if He had not called, how should we be able to believe? *For how shall they believe*, [Paul] says, *unless they do hear?* Thus the work of faith is not ours. *It is the gift*, he says, *of God*.
Saint John Chrysostom (AD 344–407),
Homilies on the Epistle to the Ephesians, 4, 2

The amazing Good News of Jesus Christ spread throughout the world in the first century. Many believed in Jesus, but others did not. Even this rejection of the Gospel was a fulfillment of prophecy. *I was ready to be found by those who did not seek me. I said, "Here am I, here am I," to a nation that did not call on my name. I spread out my hands all the day to a rebellious people, who walk in a way that is not good, following their own devices* (Isaiah 65:1–2). Whether people will accept the gracious gift of salvation Jesus offers or not, the task of evangelism remains. God can reveal Himself to seekers and to those who are not seeking Him.

Bishop Fulton J. Sheen (1895–1979) had a weekly radio audience of four million people listening to "The Catholic Hour" from 1930–1950. Later his prime time television show "Life Is Worth Living," in which he proclaimed the Gospel and explained Catholic Church teaching, attracted thirty million weekly viewers. On his television blackboard, he wrote JMJ (*Jesus, Mary, Joseph*), invoking the Holy Family to guide him.

Like Saint Paul, Bishop Sheen felt compelled to share the Good News with anyone who would listen. Many unbelieving listeners came to know Jesus through Bishop Sheen and entered the Catholic Church, including automaker Henry Ford II, former communists Louis Budenz and Bella Dodd, violinist and composer Fritz Kreisler, politician Clare Booth Luce, and other entertainers and celebrities, who each received about twenty-five hours of personal instruction from him. Countless others heard the Gospel on radio or television and sought out instruction from their neighborhood parish priest. Bishop Sheen spent an hour before the Blessed Sacrament each day and died in the presence of the Blessed Sacrament he loved.

1. What is Paul doing in Romans 10:1?

Romans 10:1
CCC 2632
CCC 2636

2. What should zeal for God achieve?

Romans 10:2–3
CCC 579

3. How does the moral law find its fulfillment?

Romans 10:4
CCC 1953
CCC 1977

4. Compare the following passages.

Deuteronomy 30:11–15
Romans 10:5–8

5. Who descended into the abyss, and why?

Romans 10:7
CCC 635
CCC 636

6. Where is the word of God? Romans 10:8

7. What must you confess?

Romans 10:9a
CCC 14

8. What must you believe? Romans 10:9b

9. What results from this faith and confession? Romans 10:10

10. Explain the significance of the name of Jesus. CCC 2666

* When have you, and when do you, profess your faith?

11. Can anyone proclaim the Gospel to himself or herself?

| Romans 10:14–15 |
| CCC 875 |

* How did you first learn about the Gospel?

12. Who is your favorite preacher or teacher of the Gospel? Romans 10:15

13. Compare the following verses.

| Isaiah 52:7 |
| Romans 10:15 |

14. Define "faith."

| Romans 10:17 |
| CCC 26 |

** If you were asked to share your faith, what would you say?

15. Describe some aspects of Christian faith.

CCC 142	
CCC 143	
CCC 150	

16. What gift is required for faith? CCC 153

17. Complete Paul's word puzzle. Romans 10:14–16

How are men to _____ upon _____ whom they have not _____?

How are they to _____ in _____ of whom they have never _____?

How are they to _____ without a _____?

How can they _____ unless they are _____?

18. Use a dictionary or the Catechism to define "evangelism."

19. How can lay people fulfill their prophet mission? CCC 905

20. When and how have you shared the Good News of Jesus Christ?

* Brainstorm ways to evangelize. Pray for opportunities to evangelize.

CHAPTER **11**

Salvation for All
Romans 11

O the depth of the riches and wisdom and knowledge of God!
How unsearchable are his judgments and how inscrutable his ways!
"For who has known the mind of the Lord,
or who has been his counselor?"
Romans 11:33–34

God's covenant with Israel holds. *I ask then, has God rejected his people? By no means! I myself am an Israelite, a descendant of Abraham, a member of the tribe of Benjamin. God has not rejected his people whom he foreknew* (Romans 11:1–3). In Romans 4, Paul recalled the faith of Father Abraham, and now he illustrates God's faithfulness in saving Abraham's sons, including Paul. The Jews were, are, and forever will be God's Chosen People. *I have loved you with an everlasting love, therefore I have continued my faithfulness to you* (Jeremiah 31:3).

While in exile, the Jews feared that God may have forsaken and abandoned them. But God spoke through the prophet Isaiah: *"Can a woman forget her suckling child, that she should have no compassion on the son of her womb? Even these may forget, yet I will not forget you"* (Isaiah 49:15). God made a covenant with Abraham that he would bless Abraham's descendants forever. Israel has been unfaithful to God, time and time again, throughout history, forsaking the One True God for idols. Yet God remains faithful. God is true to his word. God will never break his covenant with Israel or forget his promises to Abraham.

God promised David: *"I will raise up your offspring after you, who shall come forth from your body. . . . I will establish the throne of his kingdom for ever. I will be his father, and he shall be my son. When he commits iniquity, I will chasten him with the rod of men; but I will not take my merciful love away from him. . . . [Y]our throne shall be established for ever"* (2 Samuel 7:12–16). The Son of David, Jesus Christ, the King of Kings, reigns forever. When Jezebel murdered the prophets in Elijah's time (1 Kings 18–19), God preserved a remnant of the faithful prophets. Now God saves a remnant of Israel, chosen by grace (Romans 11:5).

"If salvation is by grace," someone will say, "why is it that we are not all saved?" Because you did not will it; for grace, even though it be grace, saves the willing, not those who are not willing and who turn away from it and who constantly fight against it and oppose themselves to it.
Saint John Chrysostom (AD 344–407),
Homilies on the Epistle to the Romans, 18, 5

Why has Israel failed to accept the mercy of God? Why have only the elect few recognized and accepted Jesus, the Promised Messiah? Why have so many Jewish hearts become hardened to the Good News? Paul will appeal to something that observant Jews will recognize, as he brings forth images from the *Tanakh*.

TANAKH

(A Hebrew acronym for the three divisions of the Masoretic Texts)

<u>T</u>orah—Teaching (Books of Moses)

<u>N</u>evi'im—Prophets

<u>K</u>etuvim—Writings

Paul gathers images with a common thread (*gezerah shawah*)—that of *stupor* and *loss of sight*, one verse from each of these three major divisions of the Hebrew Scriptures. In comprising Romans 11:8–10, he references 1) Isaiah the prophet, 2) Deuteronomy, the fifth book of Moses's Torah, and 3) a Psalm from the Writings, to illustrate why some fail to see the Promised Messiah, their means of salvation.

"God gave them <u>a spirit of stupor, eyes that should not see</u> and ears that should not hear, down to this very day."	*For the L*ORD *has poured out upon you <u>a spirit of deep sleep</u>, and has <u>closed your eyes</u>.* (Isaiah 29:10).
And David says, *"Let their feast become a snare and a trap, a pitfall and a retribution for them; <u>let their eyes be darkened so that they cannot see</u>."* (Romans 11:8–10).	*But to this day the L*ORD *has not given you a mind to understand, or <u>eyes to see</u>, or ears to hear.* (Deuteronomy 29:4). *<u>Let their eyes be darkened, so that they cannot see</u>.* (Psalm 69:23).

Israel stumbles on the cornerstone. God promised through the prophet Isaiah that he would send a cornerstone. *"Behold, I am laying in Zion for a foundation a stone, a tested stone, a precious cornerstone, of a sure foundation: 'He who believes will not be in haste'"* (Isaiah 28:16). Saint Peter reveals that Jesus is the cornerstone who will be rejected: *"A stone that will make men stumble and a rock that will make them fall"* (1 Peter 2:8). Sometimes a runner in a race will trip and fall, but then get up and finish the race. So too, some Jews may slip and fall, but get up and finish the race along with Saint Paul and other Jewish believers.

While the Jews stumble, the Gentiles are able to get into the race. Now, non-Jewish believers are able to share in Israel's privileged status as children of God. Paul identifies his calling as the apostle to the Gentiles. He hopes that his ministry will make some of his fellow Jews jealous and thus save some of them (Romans 11:14). Paul believes that the Jews' acceptance of the Gospel will mean *life from the dead* (Romans 11:15). Baptismal imagery comes to mind. The catechumen is plunged into water. He dies to sin, dies with Christ, in order to rise from the water, freed from original sin, to live with Christ. Also recall Ezekiel's vision of the *Valley of Dry Bones* (Ezekiel 37), in which dry bones came back to life when Ezekiel prophesied over them. Eschatological imagery points to the last days and the resurrection of the dead, when souls will be reunited with their bodies for all eternity.

The olive tree unites Jews and Gentiles. Paul offers the imagery of an olive tree to illustrate how God is bringing the believers into his fold. The *root* of the olive tree is Judaism. The root of Judaism supports Christianity. The *natural branches* are the Jewish people. The *wild olive shoots grafted on* are the non-Jewish believers. Some branches are broken off because of unbelief. Gentile believers have a dependent relationship to Israel, and they are invited to share in the blessings and graces of the Chosen People, as sons and daughters of God. The non-Jewish believer stands in awe and humility at God's gracious gift of salvation. If a believer becomes proud and haughty and falls into sin, he or she may be cut off.

Paul's word clearly refutes the "once saved, always saved" theology of some, who promise that a believer cannot lose his or her salvation, once he or she makes a commitment to Christ. *For if God did not spare the natural branches, neither will he spare you. Note then the kindness and the severity of God: severity toward those who have fallen, but God's kindness to you, provided you continue in his kindness; otherwise you too will be cut off* (Romans 11:21–22). God's perfect mercy and perfect justice are a mystery. Believers must remain faithful, humble, and repentant. God has given free will and the grace for salvation. What God has freely given, humans can freely reject. Faith and salvation are precious gifts. Jesus has given the Sacrament of Reconciliation to return to Him quickly after a fall into sin.

All Israel will be saved. *When* all Israel will be saved remains a mystery. Nevertheless, recall the words of the prophet Isaiah. *Behold, the LORD's hand is not shortened, that it cannot save. . . . "And he will come to Zion as Redeemer, to those in Jacob who turn from transgression, says the LORD. And as for me, this is my covenant with them, says the LORD: my spirit which is upon you, and my words which I have put in your mouth, shall not depart out of your mouth, or out of the mouth of your children, or out of the mouth of your children's children, says the LORD, from this time forth and for evermore"* (Isaiah 59:1, 20–21).

God's covenant with Israel cannot be revoked. The New Covenant will incorporate believers of all the nations into the Chosen People of God. God promised Abraham: *"Behold, my covenant is with you, and you shall be the father of a multitude of nations"* (Genesis 17:4). Jacob prophesied to his grandson Ephraim that *his descendants shall become a multitude of nations* (Genesis 48:19). Isaiah had visions of nations blessing Israel. *You shall eat the wealth of the nations, and in their riches you shall glory* (Isaiah 61:6). Perhaps Isaiah refers to spiritual riches and spiritual blessings will pass from the Gentiles to the Jews who will again taste God's mercy.

Saint Augustine reads *all Israel* to represent the Church, comprised of believing Jews and Gentiles, who have come to faith in Jesus and accepted baptism. Saint John Chrysostom sees *all Israel* literally as the entire race of the sons of Jacob, who will be saved and converted to Christ by the end of the age. Today there are more Jewish Christians on earth than at any other time in history. Catholics pray for the Jewish people to receive the grace to come to know Jesus Christ, the Jewish Messiah.

Be grateful to God and humble. Three times, Paul warns believers not to boast or become proud, but to remain grateful, humble, and in awe of God's kindness.

➢ *Do not boast* (Romans 11:18).
➢ *Do not become proud, but stand in awe* (Romans 11:20).
➢ *Lest you be wise in your own conceits* (Romans 11:25).

Repentant believers taste God's mercy. Wisely and humbly, penitents avoid experiencing God's severe justice. God has the power to cut one off or to graft one back in. Pride, a stumbling block, leads to peril. Fear of the Lord, a gift of the Holy Spirit, enables one to bask with reverence in the face of divine mercy and justice.

Closing prayer and hymn—*O the depth of the riches and wisdom and knowledge of God! How unsearchable are his judgments and how inscrutable is ways! "For who has known the mind of the Lord, or who has been his counselor?" "Or who has given a gift to him that he might be repaid?" For from him and through him and to him are all things. To him be glory for ever. Amen* (Romans 11:33–36).

Debra Rosenstein attained her Jewish identity from her devout Jewish grandparents, the practice of Jewish customs and the study of the Torah, which culminated in her Bat Mitzvah at age thirteen. One snowy night in high school, her eighteen-year-old brother was killed suddenly in a violent car accident, on his way home from college. Her faith, expressed primarily through customs and traditions, now at best seemed shallow.

Later, at the University of Michigan, Deb met Christians for the first time. She didn't know anything about Jesus or their religion, but she did know their beliefs were off-limits to her as a Jew. A friend invited her to watch the movie *Jesus of Nazareth*, and something both alarming and intriguing became evident—Jesus was a Jew! In an amazing scene, Jesus called His dead friend Lazarus to come out of his tomb. Could there be something after death? Could Jesus be the Jewish Messiah? Late that night Deb spoke to a God she wasn't even sure existed: "God if you are real, if Jesus is the Messiah, show me, and give me the faith to believe." That prayer for faith was answered. Now a Jewish Catholic, Debbie and Peter Herbeck are the parents of four children. She is the founder of *Be Love Revolution* and has worked for over thirty-five years to evangelize and mentor young women.

1. How does God feel about Israel?

2 Samuel 7:10
Psalm 89:2–3
Sirach 47:22
Isaiah 43:1–3
Romans 11:1–2

2. What did God tell Elijah? 1 Kings 19:10–18

3. What does God do for His people?

Genesis 45:7
Micah 2:12
Romans 11:5

4. Use a dictionary to define "remnant."

5. By what means is the remnant chosen? Romans 11:5–6

6. Why do some fail to obtain the grace of salvation? Romans 11:7

7. Find common themes in these verses.

Deuteronomy 29:4
Psalm 69:23
Isaiah 29:10
Romans 11:8–10

8. What good result comes from Israel's failure?

Romans 11:11–15
CCC 674

9. Find some hope in these verses.

Luke 15:20–24
Luke 15:32
Romans 11:15

* Have you ever felt like the Prodigal Son, the older brother, or the father?

10. Explain life after death

John 6:40
John 6:44
John 6:51
Romans 11:15

11. What is the holy root of the tree? Romans 11:15, CCC 60

12. Who are the parts of the olive tree? Romans 11:16–24

Root—
Wild olive shoots grafted on—
Broken off branches—

13. How does the Church explain this imagery? CCC 755

14. Why were olive shoots grafted in? Romans 11:17

15. Why were branches broken off? Romans 11:20

16. Find a warning that Paul gives three times. Romans 11:18, 20b, 25

17. Identify two opposite characteristics of God. Romans 11:22

18. Find a verse to refute "once saved, always saved." Romans 11:20–23

19. What reason can Paul give that "all Israel will be saved?"

Isaiah 59:20–21
Jeremiah 31:31–33
Romans 11:26

20. Choose a favorite verse from the closing hymn Romans 11:33ff or sing it.

* What is your favorite song of praise to the Lord?

CHAPTER 12

New Life in Christ
Romans 12

Do not be conformed to this world
but be transformed by the renewal of your mind,
that you may prove what is the will of God,
what is good and acceptable and perfect.
Romans 12:2

At this point, Paul transitions from dogmatic theology to moral theology. Up until now, in the Letter of Paul to the Romans, he has been giving doctrinal formation. Now Paul shifts from explaining Christian doctrine to giving a more pastoral exhortation, including practical instructions for living the Christian life. Once believers understand what Jesus has accomplished in reconciling sinful humanity, both Jews and Gentiles, to right relationship with the perfect, holy, and righteous God, then they need to understand how to live in this New Covenant with God.

Sacrifice is the highest form of adoration to God. In the Old Covenant, the priest would offer the life of a victim animal in the name of the people to show God's supreme dominion and humanity's total dependence upon God. Usually, a ram, lamb, goat, or pigeon would be killed. Blood would be poured out as an offering, and then the animal or bird would be burned on the altar. This sacrifice was offered to God in atonement for sins, in supplication for good weather or an abundant harvest or in thanksgiving for blessings received. An *oblation* offers something to God, whereas a *sacrifice* immolates or totally gives up what is presented to God. The bloody animal sacrifices in the Temple in Jerusalem came to an end when Jerusalem was sacked and the Temple destroyed in AD 70.

The prophet Micah foretold the inadequacy of those sacrifices. *"Will the LORD be pleased with thousands of rams, with ten thousands of rivers of oil? Shall I give my first-born for my transgression, the fruit of my body for the sin of my soul? He has showed you, O man, what is good, and what does the LORD require of you but to do justice, and to love kindness, and to walk humbly with your God"* (Micah 6:7–8). God *did* give His firstborn, only-begotten Son Jesus in atonement for all of the sins of the whole world. At the Last Supper, Jesus explained the perfect sacrifice: *"This is my body which is given for you. . . . This chalice which is poured out for you is the new covenant in my blood"* (Luke 22:19–20).

> **The perfect sacrifice was Christ's death on the cross; by this sacrifice, Christ accomplished our redemption as high priest of the new and eternal covenant.**

Christian, offer your body as a sacrifice, an act of worship to God. *I appeal to you therefore, brethren, by the mercies of God, to present your bodies as a living sacrifice, holy and acceptable to God, which is your spiritual worship* (Romans 12:1). How exactly does one do that? The animal sacrifices of the Old Covenant were killed, and they stayed dead. Jesus died, but rose again from the tomb alive. So, in baptism, the believer dies to sin, dies in Christ, in order to live in grace and mercy. *Do you not know that your bodies are members of Christ? . . . Do you not know that your body is a temple of the Holy Spirit within you, which you have from God* (1 Corinthians 6:15, 19)? The mercy shown to the believer must be shared with others. So to act justly, to show kindness and mercy, and to walk humbly with God become the marks of a Christian and the fulfillment of the exhortation of Micah. In the Morning Offering prayer, Catholics offer to Almighty God all their prayers, works, joys, and sufferings of the day.

Be transformed by the renewal of your mind. *Do not be conformed to this world but be transformed by the renewal of your mind, that you may prove what is the will of God, what is good and acceptable and perfect* (Romans 12:2). The world of Paul's time was an ugly and violent place—slavery, concubines and prostitutes, exposure of unwanted infants to death (usually baby girls left to die), rampant homosexual activity, vengeance, beheadings, and crucifixions. Jesus came into that darkness to bring light and life: *"I am the light of the world; he who follows me will not walk in darkness, but will have the light of life"* (John 8:12). Jesus models how to behave. Jesus demonstrates what Christians should do.

Minds and hearts are affected by the culture in which they live. In a good culture, it is easy to be good. In a wicked and dark culture, it is easy to be bad. Saint John cautions: *Do not love the world or the things in the world. If any one loves the world, love for the Father is not in him. For all that is in the world, the lust of the flesh and the lust of the eyes and the pride of life, is not of the Father but is of the world* (1 John 2:15–16). In order to ward off the temptations of the world, the flesh, and the devil, the Christian needs to have a transformed mind as well as a well-formed and enlightened conscience. People want to fit in with the crowd—to be accepted, liked, and admired. Christianity is countercultural. It may not be easy to live as a good Catholic, but it is profitable to die as a devout Catholic.

One way to evaluate whether one's mind is conformed to Christ or to the world is to look at one's time, talent, and treasure. It may be enlightening for a Christian to keep a record for a week to determine how he or she is spending time, talent, and treasure. If a person spends one hour a week in Mass on Sunday and twenty hours a week watching television, what is forming that person's mind? The busy person who feels too busy to pray may be too busy. Period. The busy person who takes time in the morning to pray often finds that much more is accomplished than seemed possible. The person who reads devotional or inspirational materials is forming his mind much differently from one who reads trashy novels or frivolous magazines. Take a week and write down how much time you spend sleeping, working, praying, eating, exercising, reading, shopping, doing chores, and enjoying sports, hobbies, leisure, and service activities. Be honest. A Christian life should be balanced. Prayer, study, and service to others should be hallmarks of an integrated life. Are there areas in which you might want to make changes? How much time do you give to God? How much time do you invest in serving others? How much time do you spend on *yourself*? What can you learn from this exercise?

Humble service breaks pride. *For by the grace given to me I bid every one among you not to think of himself more highly than he ought to think, but to think with sober judgment . . . do not be haughty . . . never be conceited* (Romans 12:3, 16). Three times in this chapter, Paul warns against vanity, arrogance, and haughtiness. *Pride goes before destruction, and a haughty spirit before a fall* (Proverbs 16:18). The virtue of humility is beautiful to behold, but not in overabundance today. Keep a healthy, modest, honest assessment of yourself. *The beginning of man's pride is to depart from the Lord; his heart has forsaken his Maker. . . . [G]lorify yourself with humility, and ascribe to yourself honor according to your worth* (Sirach 10:12, 28).

Christian life is liturgical and communal. God assigns various gifts to believers according to His grace so that believers can serve one another with *agape* (self-giving) love. Seven gifts for service are listed in Romans 12:6–8.

Gifts for Service

Prophecy—speaking divine words from God

Service—helpful acts of kindness for others

Teaching—instructing the ignorant

Exhortation—counseling and encouraging another to repent of sin

Generosity—contributing financial resources

Liberality—giving aid with zeal

Works of Mercy—feeding the hungry, giving drink to the thirsty,
clothing the naked, sheltering the homeless,
visiting the sick and imprisoned,
burying the dead

Paul lists direct, clear, specific marks of a Christian, which can be observed and measured, providing an excellent examination of conscience, in Romans 12:9–13.

✓ Is your love genuine or superficial?
✓ Do you hate evil and hold fast to what is good?
✓ Do you call a mortal sin a personal preference?
✓ Do you greet others with fraternal affection?
✓ Do you show honor, affirm, and encourage others?
✓ Are you aglow with the Spirit, serving the Lord with zeal and joy?
✓ Do you rejoice in hope?
✓ Are you patient in trials, tribulation, and suffering?
✓ Are you constant and faithful in prayer?
✓ Do you contribute generously to the needs of others?
✓ Do you offer hospitality?

Jesus described the kingdom of heaven in the beatitudes in the Sermon on the Mount. *"Blessed are those who are persecuted for righteousness sake, for theirs is the kingdom of heaven. Blessed are you when men revile you and persecute you and utter all kinds of evil against you falsely on my account"* (Matthew 5:10–11). Paul elaborates on Jesus' teaching. He tells people to bless their persecutors, to repay evil with good, and not to seek vengeance, which belongs to the Lord. The Christian should live in harmony with others, demonstrating humble service and empathy.

What does *New Life in Christ* look like? How should believers act in a dark and sinful culture? In 1998, Planned Parenthood opened an abortion clinic in Bryan/College Station, Texas. Some young Christians started to pray, but the dream of ending abortion seemed hopeless. The situation just kept getting worse and worse, as more and more women walked into Planned Parenthood for abortions.

One day in 2004, Shawn Carney and David Bereit sat at a round table and prayed for an hour. After prayer, the idea of 40 days came to them. They recruited some local volunteers and began the first ever *40 Days for Life* campaign. They offered God their peaceful prayer and fasting, around the clock, 960 continuous hours, rain or shine. As a result of this effort, they saw a 28% drop in abortions in their area. Soon, *40 Days for Life* campaigns started in 769 other cities in 50 nations. 750,000 volunteers fast and pray in front of abortion clinics. As a result, 15,256 abortions have been cancelled, enabling those thousands of babies to live.

Shawn, David, and their friends prayed for the birth mothers, for the babies, and also for the abortion workers. From the sidewalk, they spoke with the women going into the clinics, assuring them of their prayers. Over the years, hundreds of abortion workers have left the abortion industry, and 100 abortion clinics closed.

Abby Johnson, clinic director in Texas, was herself post-abortive. Shawn and his wife Marilisa prayed for her and befriended her. After actually witnessing an abortion, Abby left the abortion industry, sought out Shawn for help and started a ministry to help abortion workers who want to leave, called "And Then There Were None." Abby Johnson repented, accepted God's grace and mercy, and was received into the Catholic Church. Her autobiography, *Unplanned*, is now a movie. Shawn and David presented a problem to God, prayed, listened, and obeyed. With prayer, fasting, and peaceful sidewalk counseling, they pushed back the darkness. They offered themselves to God in a sacrifice of praise, with amazing results.

	Sunday	Monday	Tuesday	Wednesday	Thursday	Friday	Saturday
7:00 a							
8:00							
9:00							
10:00							
11:00							
Noon							
1:00 p							
2:00							
3:00							
4:00							
5:00							
6:00							
7:00							
8:00							
9:00							

1. Keep a log of how you spend your time for an entire week and evaluate it.

      ____ Time spent in prayer
      ____ Time spent in studying God's Word
      ____ Time spent serving God and others
      ____ Time for exercise and leisure
     * Where would you like to make changes?

2. Explain spiritual worship.

Romans 12:1
CCC 2031

3. What can you learn from the following passages?

Romans 12:2
1 John 2:15–17
CCC 2826

4. Define and explain "conscience."

CCC 1777
CCC 1778
CCC 1780

5. What virtue is hidden in Romans 12:3?

6. How can you grow in this virtue?

Psalm 25:4–5, 9
Sirach 2:17
Sirach 3:17–18

7. What happens for a person with this virtue? Sirach 35:16–17

8. Explain the body of Christ.

Romans 12:3–6
CCC 1142
CCC 1372

9. How should a believer use spiritual gifts?

Romans 12:3–8
1 Peter 4:10–11

10. Find and define seven spiritual gifts in Romans 12:6–8.

Prophecy	*Speaking God's Word to another—divine revelation*

11. Circle one gift above that you have and explain how you use this gift.

12. Underline a gift that you would like to develop and make a plan to do so.

13. What can you learn about love from these passages?

Romans 12:9–10
1 Corinthians 13

14. What does the Catechism teach about love?

CCC 1823
CCC 1971, 1972

15. How could you apply Romans 12:11?

16. List five commands from Romans 12:12–13.

17. What did Jesus command in Luke 6:28, and Paul repeat in Romans 12:14?

18. How can you show empathy? Romans 12:15

19. Describe the vice to be avoided from these verses.

Proverbs 3:7
Romans 12:16

20. How should you respond to evil? Romans 12:17, 21

Monthly Social Activity

This month, your small group will meet for coffee, tea, or a simple breakfast, lunch, or dessert in someone's home. Pray for this social event and for the host or hostess. Try, if at all possible, to attend.

Think about the ways in which you spend your time. Is your life in balance? Do you have time for prayer every day? Do you make time to listen to the Lord? Do you exercise and eat properly? Share with your group how you have made some successful changes.

Some examples:

❊ *I started going for a walk the first thing in the morning. While walking, I pray my rosary. I needed more exercise and more prayer, so I improved in both areas.*

❊ *Every day, I take 15 minutes to pray in the morning and 15 minutes to pray before bed.*

❊ *I was watching too much television and spending too much time on the Internet. So, I decided to limit my media time and set aside time for some spiritual reading.*

CHAPTER 13

Love One Another
Romans 13

Owe no one anything, except to love one another;
for he who loves his neighbor has fulfilled the law.
Romans 13:8

Respect governmental authorities. *Let every person be subject to the governing authorities. For there is no authority except from God and those that exist have been instituted by God* (Romans 13:1). Perhaps the first biblical evidence of the need for institutional governance appears in the Garden of Eden, after Adam and Eve disobeyed God and fell into sin. God placed *cherubim, and a flaming sword, which turned every way, to guard the way to the tree of life* (Genesis 3:24). Someone needs to maintain order and provide for the common good. Throughout history kings, judges, dictators, and elected leaders have governed. Some have ruled wisely and fairly; others were wicked and cruel. In any event, someone must take authority, and, ultimately, God will judge everyone.

It is not difficult to determine what would be the form and character of the State, were it governed according to the principles of Christian philosophy. Man's natural instinct moves him to live in civil society, for he cannot, if dwelling apart, provide himself with the necessary requirements of life, nor procure the means of developing his mental and moral faculties. Hence, it is divinely ordained that he should lead his life—be it family, or civil—with his fellow men, amongst whom alone his several wants can be adequately supplied. But, as no society can hold together unless some one be over all, directing all to strive earnestly for the common good, every body politic must have a ruling authority, and this authority, no less than society itself, has its source in nature, and has, consequently, God for its Author. Hence, it follows that all public power must proceed from God. For God alone is the true and supreme Lord of the world. Everything, without exception, must be subject to Him, and must serve him, so that whosoever holds the right to govern holds it from one sole and single source, namely, God, the sovereign Ruler of all. *There is no power but from God* (Romans 13:1).
Pope Leo XIII (AD 1810–1903), *Immortale Dei,* November 1, 1886, 3

When a civil government aligns itself in accordance with God's laws, there can be harmony among peoples and nations. When authorities ignore God's law and supremacy, ugly things happen, and the results are predictable. History repeats itself, over and over. The oppressed become oppressors. Cruel tyrants and dictators die like everyone else, to face their final judgment from a perfect and holy Judge.

Perhaps the people in the first century expected that Jesus would return very soon, and therefore, they need not pay taxes or exercise their civic responsibilities. How easy it would be to sit back and wait for the Lord to come in glory! But Paul exhorts believers to be good citizens, to obey the authorities, and to pay their taxes. Christians show honor and respect to all legitimate authorities—parents, teachers, pastors, employers, police officers, and government leaders.

Jesus said, *"Render therefore to Caesar the things that are Caesar's, and to God the things that are God's"* (Matthew 22:21). Jesus concedes that the government is entitled to collect taxes. But what are the things that belong to God? Obviously, everything that God created belongs to Him, including every human person created in His image and likeness. So to offer your body to God, as a living sacrifice (Romans 12:1), is simply to give back to God what is His due.

In front of Pontius Pilate, Jesus revealed the source of power for governmental authorities and rulers. Pilate said, *"Do you not know that I have power to release you, and power to crucify you?" Jesus answered him, "You would have no power over me unless it had been given you from above"* (John 19:11). Civil authorities are given power by God, and they will ultimately be answerable to God for the ways in which they exercised their rule and power.

> Authority is exercised legitimately only when it seeks the common good of the group concerned and if it employs morally licit means to attain it. If rulers were to enact unjust laws or take measures contrary to the moral order, such arrangements would not be binding in conscience.
>
> CCC 1903

Just laws take a concern for the common good, respecting the dignity of the human person, to achieve social well-being and peace. Christians obey civil laws. But, when a civil law directly contradicts a law of God, especially the Ten Commandments, then God's law trumps civil law. Saint Peter answered the leaders, *"Whether it is right in the sight of God to listen to you rather than to God, you must judge, for we cannot but speak of what we have seen and heard"* (Acts 4:39). Christians obey the law until it opposes God's directive. Obedience to God surpasses all else. God's law commands: *"You shall not kill"* (Exodus 20:13). Civil law permits the abortion of an innocent unborn child. God's law directs people to choose life and to protect the weak and vulnerable. Abortion, pornography, gambling, and cohabitation may be legal, but are they moral? Civil law does not have the power to convert an inherent evil into a good—a right. Sin is sin.

Love one another. It is far easier to love friends than enemies. Sometimes close family members may be difficult to love. But God does not allow exceptions. If a friend or family member is violent or abusive, one may need to forgive them, separate oneself, bring family members to safety, and then love them by praying for them from afar. Staying a safe distance away does not give one license to hate or to repay evil with evil. The Christian response requires kindness and love. Sometimes a parent must exercise "tough love" in disciplining a child. A parent takes away privileges or metes out punishment, while at the same time speaking the truth in love. An undisciplined child can become an unruly adult. Just as the Lord disciplines those He loves, parents discipline the children they love. *For the moment all discipline seems painful rather than pleasant; later it yields the peaceful fruit of righteousness to those who have been trained by it* (Hebrews 12:11).

The deeds of men are only discerned by the root of charity. For many things may be done that have a good appearance, and yet proceed not from the root of charity. For thorns also have flowers: some actions truly seem rough, seem savage; howbeit they are done for discipline at the bidding of charity. Once for all, then, a short precept is given: **Love, and do what you will:** whether you hold your peace, through love hold your peace; whether you cry out, through love cry out; whether you correct, through love correct; whether you spare, through love spare: let the root of love be within, of this root can nothing spring but what is good.

Saint Augustine of Hippo (AD 354–430),
Homily VII on the Letter of John, 8

Love and do what you will. First, obey God's commands. Do not commit adultery. Do not kill. Do not steal. Do not covet. All of the commandments can be summed up in the golden rule: Do unto others what you would have them do to you. You may be surprised to find this verse back in the Old Testament. God said, *"You shall love your neighbor as yourself: I am the* LORD*"* (Leviticus 19:18). Jesus repeated this commandment to the Rich Young Man: *"You shall love your neighbor as yourself"* (Matthew 19:19). If you love your spouse, you honor your vows and do not cheat. If you love the child in the womb, you will not cooperate with abortion. If you love your neighbor, you will not covet or steal his belongings. If you truly love others, you will not hurt them. Then you are free to do what you wish.

"You shall love the Lord your God will all your heart, and with all your soul, and with all your mind. This is the great and first commandment. And a second is like it, You shall love your neighbor as yourself. On these two commandments depend all the law and the prophets" (Matthew 22:37–40). Jesus gives a clear, simple directive on how to fulfill the law and the prophets. Saint Paul elaborates on this message and inverts it. *Love does no wrong to a neighbor; therefore love is the fulfillment of the law* (Romans 13:10). First, do no harm, do no evil. Next, do something good and beautiful for God. It is not enough to be passive; love is more than an emotion. Love is a decision, an act of the will, a giving of self for the good of others.

Saint John of the Cross said, "at the end of our lives, we will be judged on love!" That may be shocking. While obeying all of the commandments and conforming our lives to the will of God, we look at the crucifix to behold the most perfect act of love. How well do you love? Selfishness appears to be the default in contemporary culture. Love is countercultural. Love involves more than sappy emotionalism. It takes an act of the will to put another's needs first, to give to another what you would rather keep for yourself, to do for another what you would prefer to have done for you. The benchmark of the Cross challenges the one who wants to offer his or her body as a living sacrifice to God.

Put off deeds of darkness—drunkenness, debauchery, licentiousness, quarreling, and jealousy, and put on Jesus Christ (Romans 13:13–14). Jesus came into the darkness of our world to bring us into the light of His love. In the midst of a dark and sinful world, Jesus models the perfect example of living the truth in love. The culture around may seem evil and hopeless, but a better world awaits on the horizon.

Poland lost World War II twice—once to the brutal German Nazis, and then to the oppressive Russian Communists. Two evil regimes followed one another. The people of Poland had little hope to cling to, aside from their Catholic faith. The political situation in Poland remained bleak and oppressive.

In the midst of this darkness, God used an ordinary lay Catholic to accomplish something extraordinary and unimaginable. Lech Walesa, an electrician and shipyard worker, organized Solidarity, the first independent trade union in the Soviet bloc. He was placed under surveillance, fired from his job in 1976, and arrested and imprisoned several times, causing hardship for his wife Danuta and their eight children. And yet, Lech Walesa kept his faith and his peace.

When his fellow Pole, Pope (Saint) John Paul II came to Poland, the Pope asked the authorities for the opportunity to meet with Lech Walesa. Initially, the Communist leaders refused to allow the meeting. But, how do you say "No" to a Polish Pope who wants to visit with a fellow countryman while the whole world is watching? So they reluctantly agreed to the meeting, but only in a remote lodge in the mountains, far away from cameras. Pope John Paul II was shrewd and experienced in dealing with the Communists. He knew that the lodge would be bugged and that their conversation would be recorded and forwarded to Moscow. So, when he met with Lech, he suggested that they go for a walk in the mountains, far away from the listening ears of the oppressive tyrants.

The whole world watched in awe as the Iron Curtain fell without a single shot being fired. The Berlin Wall came down. Solidarity, the independent trade union, negotiated better working conditions for laborers. People were subsequently allowed free elections of their leaders. Lech Walesa was awarded the Nobel Peace Prize in 1983 and served as the elected President of Poland from 1990 to 1995.

Sometimes, people must put up with wicked government authorities. But, at other times, when leaders fail to rule in good faith, God may intervene

114

1. What can you learn about governmental authorities? Romans 13:1

2. How does the Catholic Church see contributing to the common good?

CCC 1906
CCC 1907
CCC 1908
CCC 1909
CCC 1910

3. What are some responsibilities of good citizens?

Romans 13:1–2, 7
CCC 2238
CCC 2239
CCC 2240

4. Explain the role of conscience in obeying laws. Romans 13:3b, CCC 2242

* Give an example of a law that you, in good conscience could disobey.

5. How do you show respect and honor? Romans 13:7b

6. What can you learn about leadership from Proverbs 8:12–17?

7. How can you fulfill the law? Romans 13:8

8. Identify these commandments and cross-reference. Romans 13:9, Exodus 20:12ff

Deuteronomy 5:17
Deuteronomy 5:18
Deuteronomy 5:19
Deuteronomy 5:21

* Which commandment is the easiest for you to obey, and which is the hardest?

9. What did God command in the Old Covenant? Leviticus 19:18

10. How can you explain the importance of keeping the law?

Matthew 19:17
Matthew 22:35–40
Romans 13:9
CCC 2196

11. What does James call this commandment? James 2:8

12. What fulfills the law? Romans 13:10

13. Compare these passages.

Romans 13:9b–10
Galatians 5:13–15

14. List five practical ways to demonstrate love to family members and neighbors.

15. What does Paul want believers to do? Romans 13:112

Ephesians 4:15
1 Thessalonians 5:6

16. What can you learn about darkness and light? Romans 13:12

John 8:12
1 John 2:8–11

17. Who helps you to live in the light? John 14:25–26

18. List some works of darkness (evil).

Romans 13:12–13
Galatians 5:19–21

19. How does one initially put on Christ?

Romans 13:14
Galatians 3:27

20. How do you stay in the light? John 15:4–9

CHAPTER 14

Do Not Judge
Romans 14

None of us lives to himself, and none of dies to himself.
If we live, we live to the Lord, and if we die, we die to the Lord;
so then, whether we live or whether we die, we are the Lord's.
Romans 14:7–8

Do not judge one another. In order to understand Romans 14, it may be helpful to imagine life for the Hebrew people in the first century. Observant Jews sought to honor God by obeying all 613 precepts of the Mosaic Law, including many kosher dietary regulations. Good Jews did not eat pork or shellfish. Jewish women served different foods on separate plates. Dairy products were not served on the same dish as meats, for example. Kosher butchers made sure that all blood was drained from slaughtered animals and that any meat from animals that had been sacrificed to idols was not consumed by Jews. This understanding provides background information for the dispute that Paul seems to be addressing.

When Jesus came, He died to reconcile all sinners, Jews and Gentiles, to Almighty God. And Jesus provided a way for Jews and Gentiles to worship together. The most holy sacrifice of the Mass contains a sacred meal—the Eucharist. Jews and Gentiles cannot receive the body, blood, soul, and divinity of the Lord if they cannot eat together. In the first century, many good Jews who accepted Jesus as the Messiah felt compelled to continue to observe the Mosaic Law, as a means of pleasing God. Certainly, this was Saint Peter's intention, until God intervened.

Once Peter went up on the housetop to pray and became very hungry. He fell into a trance and received a vision of a great sheet filled with all kinds of animals and birds, coming down from the sky. A voice invited Peter to get up, kill, and eat. But Peter refused, for he was a good Jew, and had never eaten unclean food. *And the voice came to him again a second time, "What God has cleansed, you must not call common"* (Acts 10:15). Subsequently, an angel of the Lord told the Gentile Cornelius to send for Peter. When Peter met Cornelius and heard his story, Peter realized that God had prepared Cornelius and his household to hear about Jesus and accept baptism. While Peter was evangelizing Cornelius, the Holy Spirit fell on everyone who heard Peter proclaim the Gospel and the entire household of Cornelius was baptized. Later, the brethren criticized Peter for eating with uncircumcised men. Peter reported everything to the other apostles.

Some Gentile Christians adopted ritual Jewish practices when they embraced the Gospel of Christ. And some Jewish Christians continued to obey kosher dietary laws and to observe the traditional festivals and holy days, while other Jewish Christians believed that the ritual prescriptions of the law were no longer necessary. Paul understood that each group wanted to please God in worship, but they were criticizing one another and disrupting fellowship. Note that they are not disagreeing about the Ten Commandments. No one is saying that idolatry, killing, stealing, adultery, or lying is acceptable. So the issue here does not concern a person who is objectively committing mortal sins against God. What is judgment?

Judgment—entails affirming the truth or harmony of two concepts.
"God is good" affirms the truth by agreement.
"God is not evil" also confirms the truth by contrast.
In ethics, judgment is a right decision about an act that is right, proper, or prudent.

Ultimately, God will judge. Each group that Paul addresses believes they are right and moral in their actions. The challenge for Paul is to find a charitable solution, allowing for mutual respect and acceptance that will enable the Christians to worship together. Both groups intend to honor and give thanks to God, but they do so in different ways. Perhaps a contemporary parallel would involve one Catholic who abstains from meat on Fridays in remembrance of Our Lord's Passion, while another Catholic spends an hour in Adoration of the Blessed Sacrament on Friday to recall the sufferings of Jesus. Both intend to do something pleasing to God. Neither is involved in sin, but, if they start criticizing one another, a problem arises.

None of us lives to himself, and none of us dies to himself. If we live, we live to the Lord, and if we die, we die to the Lord; so then, whether we live or whether we die, we are the Lord's. For to this end Christ died and lived again, that he might be Lord both of the dead and of the living (Romans 14:7–9). Paul recalls the death and Resurrection of Jesus, which changed the whole course of human history. Saint Peter announced to the crowd on Pentecost, *"Let all the house of Israel know assuredly that God has made him both Lord and Christ, this Jesus whom you crucified"* (Acts 2:36). Later, Peter explained to Cornelius that Jesus was appointed to ultimately judge the living and the dead. *"And he commanded us to preach to the people, and to testify that he is the one ordained by God to be judge of the living and the dead"* (Acts 10:42). The Nicene Creed proclaims that Jesus will come again to judge the living and the dead. So Christians live for Him and long for the day when He will come again and judge each individual.

When a Jew or a Gentile hears the Gospel, repents of sin, and believes in Jesus, he or she dies to Christ in Baptism, in order to live for Christ. In the Catholic funeral liturgy, mourners are comforted in hearing that because a loved one has died with Christ in Baptism, he or she can hope to rise with Christ. Paul recalls this truth in his letters to various communities. *I have been crucified with Christ; it is no longer I who live, but Christ who lives in me; and the life I now live in the flesh I live by faith in the Son of God, who loved me and gave himself for me* (Galatians 2:20). Jesus offers believers a ministry of reconciliation with God the Father and with one another. *For the love of Christ urges us on, because we are convinced that one has died for all; therefore all have died. And he died for all, that those who live might live no longer for themselves but for him who for their sake died and was raised* (2 Corinthians 5:14–15). Because Christ died for our salvation, we are brothers and sisters in Christ. Christians should not put obstacles or stumbling blocks in front of others. Christians live for Christ and avoid judging one another, unless the brother or sister falls into sin. Jesus gives clear and specific directions about sin.

"If your brother sins against you, go and tell him his fault, between you and him alone. If he listens to you, you have gained your brother. But if he does not listen, take one or two others along with you, that every word may be confirmed by the evidence of two or three witnesses. If he refuses to listen to them, tell it to the Church, and if he refuses to listen even to the Church, let him be to you as a Gentile and a tax collector" (Matthew 18:15–17). Jesus clearly exhorts believers to deal with sin. Paul also admonishes believers to deal seriously with sin in the community. *I wrote to you not to associate with any one who bears the name of brother if he is guilty of immorality or greed, or is an idolater, reviler, drunkard, or robber—not even to eat with such a one* (1 Corinthians 5:11).

In *Veritatis Splendor*, Pope (Saint) John Paul II advised Christians to evaluate the morality or immorality, goodness or evil, of given actions. Each person must consider the fundamental options available and choose.

> In point of fact, the morality of human acts is not deduced only from one's intention, orientation or fundamental option, understood as an intention devoid of a clearly determined binding content or as an intention with no corresponding positive effort to fulfill the different obligations of the moral life. Judgments about morality cannot be made without taking into consideration whether or not the deliberate choice of a specific kind of behavior is in conformity with the dignity and integral vocation of the human person. Every choice always implies a reference by the deliberate will to the goods and evils indicated by the natural law as goods to be pursued and evils to be avoided. In the case of the positive moral precepts, prudence always has the task of verifying that they apply in a specific situation, for example, in view of other duties, which may be more important or urgent. But the negative moral precepts, those prohibiting certain concrete actions or kinds of behavior as intrinsically evil, do not allow for any legitimate exception. They do not leave room, in any morally acceptable way, for the "creativity" of any contrary determination whatsoever. Once the moral species of an action prohibited by a universal rule is concretely recognized, the only morally good act is that of obeying the moral law and of refraining from the action which it forbids.
>
> Pope (Saint) John Paul II,
> *Veritatis Splendor*, August 6, 1993, 67.2–3

Jesus is the ultimate judge who will determine the final destiny of each human person at the time of his or her particular judgment on the day of death. No one should attempt to take the place of Jesus in exonerating or condemning another person. However, some people will read these verses out of context and conclude that no one should ever judge any action, which is impossible. No one sees a bully beating a child over the head and says, "Oh well, who am I to judge?" Common sense dictates that you jump in to help a vulnerable person and stop the aggressor. Remember that each person must give an account to God. On judgment day, think how would it sound to say to the Lord: "I did not want to interfere. I did not want to say anything. Who am I to judge? It was none of my business."

Jesus says clearly, *"Do not judge by appearances, but **judge with right judgment"*** (John 7:24). Jesus commands us to judge rightly. The first person to judge is oneself. Each night, many Catholics make an examen, recalling the events of the day and evaluating which thoughts and deeds were pleasing to God and which were not. The Sacrament of Reconciliation provides an excellent opportunity to regularly judge one's sinful thoughts, acts, and omissions, and to get right with God before the day of final judgment. May each person regularly receive the great gift of mercy from Jesus in Confession. And when seeing a brother or sister involved in serious sin, may God give the grace to *speak the truth in love* (Ephesians 4:15).

Paul Dawson, a high-end male model, appeared in advertisements in magazines and on billboards. Paul was introduced into the homosexual lifestyle at South Beach in Miami as a teenager. Over the years, he saw many of his gay friends in New York City die of AIDS (auto-immune deficiency syndrome). Even though Paul had engaged in the same high-risk behaviors as his friends, with numerous liaisons, he seemed unaffected. So he and his partner moved to the West coast.

New medications for HIV/AIDS were being developed and made available, and friends pressured Paul to be tested for HIV. Reluctantly, Paul was tested, and learned that he did not have HIV. At that time, he felt like he heard the Lord say that He wasn't finished with Paul yet and had work for him to do.

One night while Paul was at home channel surfing on the television, he stumbled across an elderly nun in a habit with a patch over her eye. Mother Angelica had suffered a stroke, which damaged her eye, and she wore a patch while recovering. Paul mocked her, and said to his partner, "Look at this—a pirate nun!" But he secretly started watching EWTN and listening to what this nun had to say about God's love, heaven and hell, sin and judgment, repentance, and the need for God's mercy.

Somehow Paul received the grace to recognize his sin and repent. He decided to turn to the Lord, beg for God's mercy, and try to live a chaste lifestyle. In doing so, he discovered a peace and joy that had always eluded him. Paul has been instrumental in helping other people who experience same-sex attraction to turn to Jesus for help in leading chaste and holy lives. Paul can be seen in the documentary film *Desire of the Everlasting Hills*, produced by the Courage apostolate.

1. Identify the conflict in Romans 14:1–2.

2. Use a dictionary or the catechism to define "judgment." CCC 1021–1022

3. Explain the difference between making a judgment and being judgmental.

4. Can you reconcile these apparent contradictions?

Sirach 31:15	
Matthew 7:1–2	
John 7:24	

* Explain a time when you were judged or judged another unfairly.

5. Ultimately, who has the right to judge?

CCC 678	
CCC 679	

6. Identify a risk in the following admonition.

Romans 14:3–4
CCC 2477
CCC 2478

7. What caution is given in Colossians 2:16?

8. What pleases God? Psalm 133:1–3

9. What is the end goal of all efforts? Romans 14:6

10. Compare these verses.

Romans 14:7
Galatians 2:20
2 Corinthians 5:15

11. Compare these verses.

Romans 14:8
Philippians 1:20

12. Why should you reserve judgment of another? Romans 14:10

13. Find a common thread in these verses.

Isaiah 45:22–23
Romans 14:11
Philippians 2:5–11

14. What must you do at the end of your life? Romans 14:12

* Brainstorm practical ways to prepare yourself for that event.

15. What conflict emerges again in Romans 14:13ff?

16. What stumbling blocks do Christians face today? Romans 14:13

17. Of what does the kingdom of God consist? Romans 14:17

18. What should Christians pursue? Romans 14:18–19

19. What does Jesus ask of us?

Mark 9:50
Romans 14:19

20. Explain Romans 14:22

* Identify ways that you could correct someone in sin, without condemning.

CHAPTER 15

Serve Others
Romans 15

May the God of steadfastness and encouragement
grant you to live in such harmony with one another,
in accord with Jesus Christ,
that together you may with one voice
glorify the God and Father of our Lord Jesus Christ.
Romans 15:5–6

Serve and bless others—Paul continues discussing the problem of ritual dietary regulations and observances of the Old Covenant. He refers to those who continue to respect kosher dietary laws as "weak" and to those who no longer observe ritual practices as "strong." The only apparent way to solve this conflict is for the strong to forbear with the weak. Jesus provides the example of humble service at the Last Supper, when He washes the disciples' feet. *"If I then, your Lord and Teacher, have washed your feet, you also ought to wash one another's feet. For I have given you an example, that you also should do as I have done to you"* (John 13:14–15).

Paul exhorts the Christians not to strive to please themselves, but to bear with one another and to please others in order to edify them. Christ gives many examples of bearing up with the weak in His dealings with sinners and scoffers. The leaders of the Christian community should also take a concern for the weak.

> The same rationale is observed in the declaring of one's sins as in the detection of physical diseases. Just as the diseases of the body are not divulged to all, nor haphazardly, but to those who are skilled in curing them, so too our declaration of our sins should be made to those empowered to cure them, even as it is written, *"You that are strong, bear the infirmities of the weak"* (Romans 15:1); that is, carry them by means of your diligent care.
> Saint Basil the Great (AD 330–379), *Rules Briefly Treated*, 229

When questions and disputes arise concerning worship—or any dubious personal behavior or practice—the believer can take his issue to the priest. The Sacrament of Reconciliation provides the perfect environment for the weak sinner to bring his failings into the light. The priest can discern and counsel concerning scrupulosity, as well as giving absolution and guidance for dealing with genuine, deliberate sins.

Jesus bore the insults and sins of all of humanity. Christ did not seek to please Himself, but gave Himself up for sinful people. Paul recalls the Psalm and the voice of Jesus:

the insults of those who insult you have fallen on me (Psalm 69:9b). Forbearance involves patience, self-control, and tolerance. Because God puts up with us sinners, with all of our sins and foibles, we ought to be able to forbear with our brothers and sisters, with all of their quirks and weaknesses, as well.

For whatever was written in former days was written for our instruction, that by steadfastness and by the encouragement of the Scriptures we might have hope (Romans 15:4). God gave the Law and the Prophets to guide and direct the Chosen People, until the promised Messiah would come. Hope is now fulfilled in Jesus Christ, and people continue to benefit from the instruction of the Scriptures. *All Scripture is inspired by God and profitable for teaching, for reproof, for correction, and for training in righteousness, that the man of God may be complete, equipped for every good work* (2 Timothy 3:16–17).

Harmony among brothers and sisters in worship pleases God. *May the God of steadfastness and encouragement grant you to live in such harmony with one another, in accord with Christ Jesus, that together you may with one voice glorify the God and Father of our Lord Jesus Christ* (Romans 15:5–6). Anyone who has ever visited a monastery and heard the monks or nuns singing psalms in perfect harmony will recall being drawn up into heavenly worship. Suppressing one's own personal preference allows for uniformity in liturgical worship and glorifies God.

Jews and Gentiles come to glorify God together. Once again, Paul strings a *catena* of Scripture passages together to illustrate his point: Jesus came to save everyone who is willing to believe and repent. He again references *Tanakh*—the Torah, the prophets, and the writings—to show that Christ has fulfilled the promises given to the patriarchs. Jesus came to save both the circumcised and the uncircumcised.

- ➢ Psalm 18:49   *For this I will extol you, O LORD, among the nations,*
                                    and sing praises to your name.
- ➢ 2 Samuel 22:50   *"For this I will extol you, O LORD, among the nations,*
                                    and sing praises to your name."
- ➢ Deuteronomy 32:43 *"Praise his people, O you nations;*
                                    for he avenges the blood of his servants,"
- ➢ Psalm 117:1   *Praise the Lord, all nations!*
                                    Extol him, all peoples!
- ➢ Isaiah 11:10   *In that day the root of Jesse shall stand as an ensign*
                                    to the peoples; him shall the nations seek.

Paul has explained deep, dogmatic theology and offered pastoral, moral theology. He challenged people to serve one another, to forbear with one another, and to worship the Lord in unity and harmony. Now, Paul prays for the believers. *May the God of hope fill you with all joy and peace in believing, so that by the power of the Holy Spirit you may abound in hope* (Romans 15:13). Knowing the fullness of the Gospel message and behaving in accordance with the teachings of Christ lead naturally to praying for others and sharing the Good News with people. Study God's Word, live the Scriptures, pray for others, and share the treasure.

Believers are prepared for service. Paul affirms the believers, who have obtained knowledge of Christ and goodness and now are equipped to instruct others in the faith. Jesus has come to earth and died for sinners. And, because He comes individually to each believer, Christians wait expectantly for Him to come again.

We know that there are three comings of the Lord. The third lies between the other two. It is invisible, while the other two are visible. In the first coming he was seen on earth, dwelling among men; he himself testifies that they saw him and hated him. In the final coming *all flesh will see the salvation of our God, and they will look on him whom they pierced.* The intermediate coming is a hidden one; in it only the elect see the Lord within their own selves, and they are saved. In his first coming our Lord came in our flesh and our weakness; in this middle coming he comes in spirit and in power; in the final coming he will be seen in glory and majesty. . . .

In case someone should think that what we say about this middle coming is sheer invention, listen to what our Lord himself says: *If anyone loves me, he will keep my word, and my Father will love him, and we will come to him. . . He who fears God will do good,* but something further has been said about the one who loves, that is, that he will keep God's word. Where is God's word to be kept? Obviously in the heart, as the prophet says: *I have hidden your words in my heart, so that I may not sin against you.*

Keep God's word in this way. Let it enter into your very being, let it take possession of your desires and your whole way of life. Feed on goodness, and your soul will delight in richness. Remember to eat your bread, or your heart will wither away. Fill your soul with richness and strength.

Saint Bernard, Abbot of Clairvaux, (AD 1090–1174),
Sermon 5, In Adventu Domini, 1–3

Paul identifies himself as the apostle to the Gentiles. At the beginning of this Letter to the Romans, Paul identified himself as *Paul, a servant of Jesus Christ, called to be an apostle, set apart for the gospel of God which he promised beforehand through his prophets in the holy Scriptures* (Romans 1:1–2). Now, drawing to the close of this letter, Paul provides additional biographical information about himself. *I have written to you very boldly by way of reminder, because of the grace given me by God to be a minister of Christ Jesus to the Gentiles in the priestly service of the gospel of God, so that the offering of the Gentiles may be acceptable, sanctified by the Holy Spirit. In Christ Jesus, then, I have reason to be proud of my work for God* (Romans 15:15–17).

How does one become an apostle to the Gentiles? First, Christ commissioned Paul for his work. Secondly, Paul knew the Scriptures, recalled, and proclaimed them freely and frequently. Finally, in the power of the Holy Spirit, Paul worked signs and wonders to demonstrate the power of God. Jesus worked signs and wonders to prove that He was divine. Jesus promised to give this power to His disciples. *"Truly, truly, I say to you, he who believes in me will also do the works that I do; and greater works than these will he do, because I go to the Father. Whatever you ask in my name, I will do it, that the Father may be glorified in the Son"* (John 14:12–13).

Some of the signs and wonders that Paul worked include:
- ➤ A man crippled from birth is made well (Acts 14:8–10).
- ➤ Paul exorcises a demon from a slave girl (Acts 16:16–18).
- ➤ Sick people are healed from diseases and evil spirits (Acts 19:11–12).
- ➤ Paul raises Eutychus from the dead (Acts 20:7–12).
- ➤ Paul survives a poisonous viper's bite (Acts 28:3–6).
- ➤ Many people on the island of Malta were healed of diseases (Acts 28:7–9).

Paul met Jesus and was converted on the road to Damascus. His great joy was found in telling people about Jesus, especially those who had never heard of him, in fulfillment of Isaiah's prophecy *for that which has not been told them they shall see, and that which they have not heard they shall understand* (Isaiah 52:15). Meeting Jesus along the way in one's life brings the greatest joy that anyone can imagine, and telling others about Jesus multiplies that delight.

Anne grew up in a typical family in the Midwest. She attended a Protestant church with her parents and went to Sunday school. She was a good student in school. After high school graduation, Anne was diligently working at her job when she suffered a nervous breakdown and was hospitalized.

Diagnosed with a complete psychotic breakdown, Anne endured multiple electroconvulsive therapy treatments. At that time, no one suspected that repeated shock treatments might leave the patient with serious health problems. Nonetheless, after more than twenty shock treatments, there was no improvement in her health. Soon Anne's parents had expended all of their health insurance benefits and exhausted their savings on her medical care. The doctors suggested that they take her home to wait for placement in a long-term, state run, psychiatric hospital. They could offer no hope for improvement for Anne. So she went home to wait.

While at home waiting, some friends invited Anne to go with them to a prayer meeting in the student chapel of a nearby college, where some "cute guys" played guitar and led the worship. Why not? Anne went to the prayer meeting. As soon as she heard the name "Jesus," she knew that she was instantly healed. Anne became a Catholic, and, for more than three decades, she has led a life of service to the Lord, ministering primarily to young women. Despite the fact that the doctors offered her no hope, she has not had a psychiatric treatment or hospitalization since the moment Jesus healed her at that prayer meeting in the student chapel.

1. Why should Christians defer to one another?

Psalm 69:9
John 13:3–15
Romans 15:1–3
CCC 520

2. Explain the purpose of the Scriptures.

Romans 15:4
2 Timothy 3:16–17
CCC 101
CCC 105

* How has Scripture study affected your life?

3. For what does Paul pray in these passages?

Romans 15:5–6
Philippians 2:2

4. How and why should you welcome others?

Romans 15:7–8
Hebrews 13:1–2

* Share a time when a Christian welcomed you.

5. Who did Jesus come to save, and why? Romans 15:7–9

6. What can you learn from these passages?

Deuteronomy 32:43
2 Samuel 22:50
Isaiah 11:10
Psalm 18:49; 117:1

7. How can you persevere in faith? CCC 162

** What tools help you to persevere in faith?

8. What does Paul pray for the people? Romans 15:13

9. How does Paul evaluate the people? Romans 15:14

10. What do these passages reveal about Paul and his work?

Romans 15:15
Romans 15:16
Romans 15:17

11. What was Paul's aim or purpose? Romans 15:18

12. Describe some signs and wonders that Paul worked.

Acts 14:8–10
Acts 16:16–18
Acts 19:11–12
Acts 20:7–12

* Have you ever seen a sign or wonder?

13. Who did Paul want to evangelize? Romans 15:20–21

14. What was Paul's hope? Romans 15:22–24

15. Describe the responsibility Paul must discharge. Romans 15:25–27

16. Explain the exchange in Romans 15:27.

17. How does Paul hope to arrive in Rome? Romans 15:29

18. Through whom does Paul intercede? Romans 15:30

19. For what does Paul pray in Romans 15:31–33?

20. Who teaches you how to pray? CCC 2657

* Do you have a special prayer intention right now?

Chapter 16

Relationships
Romans 16

*Now to him who is able to strengthen you according to my gospel
and the preaching of Jesus Christ,
according to the revelation of the mystery which was kept secret for long ages
but is now disclosed and through the prophetic writings
is made known to all nations, according to the command of the eternal God,
to bring about the obedience of faith—
to the only wise God be glory for evermore through Jesus Christ! Amen.*
Romans 16:25–27

Relationships help bring about the obedience of faith. Temptations may emerge to skip the final chapter of Romans, with its unfamiliar, difficult-to-pronounce names. But that would be a mistake. God's Word teaches us something important in the long genealogies and personal greetings to individual people. Jesus took on human flesh to become one of us and to save each one of us, individually and personally. Jesus did not only come to save the whole world. He came to save YOU and me! Jesus called His disciples by name. He looked up at Zacchaeus in a tree, called him by name, and visited his home (Luke 19:2–5). Jesus made friends with Martha, Mary, and Lazarus, and loved them (John 11:5). Jesus looked at individuals, called them by name, shared meals with them, and offered them new life.

Pope Benedict XVI emeritus said that being a Christian is not the result of an ethical duty or lofty idea, but *the encounter with a Person* who gives life direction—Jesus. Pope (Saint) John Paul II said that catechesis without *personal attachment to Jesus Christ* falls on deaf ears. It is only when *we fall in love with Jesus* that we truly desire to worship Him and receive His body and blood at Mass.

Saint Mother Teresa of Kolkata worried that some of her religious sisters in the Missionaries of Charity had not really met Jesus—one-to-one. She encouraged them to never give up the pursuit of this intimate contact with Jesus as a real, living person—not just an idea. If Mother Teresa was concerned about her religious sisters, who pray and nurse the destitute and dying every day, not having a personal relationship with Jesus, then no one should feel badly about not knowing Jesus as intimately as one would like. Just never give up seeking Jesus and desiring to grow ever closer to Him. Christianity is not just about rules, as important as they may be. Christianity springs from a *relationship* with God.

Major evangelistic programs, sophisticated media presentations, polished homilies, and outreaches are all essential. However, Christianity started out with one person bringing his brother, his friend, to meet Jesus. One beggar showed another beggar where the free bread was being offered. Thousands of years later, the same method works. One sinner tells another sinner how to find God's grace. A friend, neighbor, or coworker shares, "Let me tell you the amazing story of the mercy that God has shown to me." Personal relationships are vital to evangelization.

> There is a stream which flows down on God's saints like a torrent. There is also a river giving joy to the heart that is at peace and makes for peace. Whoever has received from the fullness of this river, like John the Evangelist, like Peter and Paul, lifts up his voice. Just as the apostles lifted up their voices and preached the Gospel throughout the world, so those who drink these waters begin to preach the good news of the Lord Jesus. Drink then, from Christ, so that your voice may also be heard. . . . He who reads much and understands much, receives his fill. He who is full, refreshes others.
>
> Saint Ambrose, bishop (AD 340–397), *Epistle 2, 5–5*

Paul sends personal greetings. Who are the people named in Romans 16? It is impossible to know with certainty exactly who these people are, but Scripture gives some hints about some of them. Phoebe may have been a woman of some means, who used her resources to help others in the body of Christ (Romans 16:1–2). The word for deaconess (Greek *diakonia*) can be used to mean a servant or a minister. Later in the Church, this term became used to designate a specific pastoral role and today refers to an ordained minister. But all we know for certain about Phoebe is that she was a wealthy, generous friend and helper of many.

Prisca and Aquila, a Jewish husband and wife, first met Paul in Corinth, after they had fled from Rome, possibly due to the decree from Claudius in AD 49. They first appear in the Acts of the Apostles (Acts 18:2), where Prisca is called Priscilla. They shared the same livelihood as Paul in that they were all tentmakers. Paul stayed with Prisca and Aquila there, and they worked together at their craft. Apparently, Prisca and Aquila risked their lives for Paul, and they have now returned to Rome, where they host a house church (Romans 16:3–5).

Paul greets several people as *kinsmen*. But it is unclear whether Paul uses the term *kinsmen* to mean blood relatives, members of the same region or tribe, or brothers and sisters in the faith. *Greet Andronicus and Junias, my kinsmen and my fellow prisoners; they are men of note among the apostles, and they were in Christ before me* (Romans 16:7). Whether Paul met Andronicus and Junias in prison, and whether they were imprisoned for their faith in Christ, as Paul was, we cannot determine. But it is clear that they believed in Jesus even before Paul did. So perhaps they heard Peter preach on Pentecost or accepted the faith at another time before Paul met the Lord. Perhaps they are now evangelists, as well.

Rufus is an interesting name to note, as it appears earlier in the Bible. During the way of the cross, Jesus fell several times, probably due to exhaustion and blood loss, on the way to His crucifixion. *And they compelled a passer by, Simon of Cyrene, who was coming in from the country, the father of Alexander and Rufus, to carry his cross*

(Mark 15:21). Here, Paul mentions a certain Rufus, who may, or may not, be the same man. *Greet Rufus, eminent in the Lord, also his mother and mine* (Romans 16:13). Paul seems to indicate that Rufus and his family are close to him and that the mother of Rufus has become a maternal figure to Paul, as well.

Offer the kiss of peace. *Greet one another with a holy kiss. All the churches of Christ greet you* (Romans 16:16). Even two thousand years after the time of Saint Paul, Catholics offer one another a sign of peace in the most holy sacrifice of the Mass. An infallible sign of the presence of God is the joy, warmth, and fellowship that Christians display in greeting one another, visitors, and guests.

Warning concerning dissenters and heretics—Paul cautions the believers to note and avoid those who will create problems by introducing opposing doctrines. Heretics spring up in the church very early on, and they continue to wreak havoc to this very day. Paul gives an admonition that echoes the words of Jesus. *I would have you wise as to what is good and guileless as to what is evil; then the God of peace will soon crush Satan under your feet* (Romans 16:19–20). Jesus said, *"Behold, I send you out as sheep in the midst of wolves; so be wise as serpents and innocent as doves"* (Matthew 10:16). Be on your guard against false teachers.

There is no doubt that Christian moral teaching, even in its biblical roots, acknowledges the specific importance of a fundamental choice which qualifies the moral life and engages freedom on a radical level before God. It is a question of the *obedience of faith* (Romans 16:26) *by which man makes a total and free self-commitment to God, offering "the full submission of intellect and will to God as he reveals."* This faith, which works through love (Galatians 5:6), comes from the core of man, from his *heart* (Romans 10:10), whence it is called to bear fruit in works.

The morality of the New Covenant is similarly dominated by the fundamental call of Jesus to follow him—thus he also says to the young man: *"If you wish to be perfect . . . then come, follow me"* (Matthew 19:21); to this call the disciple must respond with a radical decision and choice. The Gospel parables of the treasure and pearl of great price, for which one sells all one's possessions, are eloquent and effective images of the radical and unconditional nature of the decision demanded by the Kingdom of God. The radical nature of the decision to follow Jesus is admirably expressed in his own words: *"Whoever would save his life will lose it; and whoever loses his life for my sake and the Gospel's will save it"* (Mark 8:35).

Pope (Saint) John Paul II,
Veritatis Splendor, August 6, 1993, 66.1–2

Timothy, Paul's disciple and coworker, sends greetings, as well. When Paul traveled to Derbe and Lystra, he met Timothy, who was the son of a Jewish Christian mother and a Greek father. Interestingly, Paul circumcised Timothy before allowing him to accompany him on mission (Acts 16:1–5). The scribe Tertius identifies himself as the person who penned Paul's letter (Romans 16:22). Paul recognizes his host Gaius, who provides hospitality for Paul, while he is in Corinth.

Paul's final doxology brings the reader back to where he began, aiming to bring about *the obedience of faith*. The obedience of faith references in Romans 1:5 and Romans 16:26 serve as bookends, a framing device to highlight his theme.

Paul started by proclaiming God's righteousness, contrasted to the wickedness of sinful humanity, and the clear evidence of God's perfect goodness. The uncircumcised, as well as God's chosen people, have failed to honor God. Hence, Paul showed that everyone needs a Savior. Each person, Jew and Gentile, chooses between continuing in slavery to sin or believing in Jesus Christ and accepting the grace of justification that comes through faith in Him.

While affirming the privileged place of the Jewish people and their primacy in election, Paul proclaimed Jesus as the Messiah and Savior of the whole world. He showed the practical ways in which sinners receive God's grace and respond to the leadings of the Holy Spirit. After his conversion, Paul spent his whole life drawing people into a radical relationship with Jesus and encouraging the obedience of faith.

The same challenge remains today. God is perfect in holiness and righteousness. He has revealed Himself in nature and in the person of his only begotten Son Jesus. By His sacrifice and death on the cross, Jesus reconciles sinful humanity to God. In His Resurrection, Jesus proves that He is God, with dominion over sin and death. When a sinner repents of his sin and accepts Baptism, he is justified and at peace with God. Then the Holy Spirit comes to provide the grace to live a life in obedience to faith. Christians worship God with others in the Church, until Jesus comes again in glory. The Good News that Paul shared remains the best news for people today.

Paul Vitz was an atheist in college, studying psychology at the University of Michigan and completing his PhD at Stanford in California, in the era of "sex, drugs, and rock and roll." He became a professor at New York University in 1965 and encountered civil rights, women's rights, and gay rights movements all trying to remake the world into a better place. He fell in love and married Timmie, but he was filled with anxiety. Marriage and fatherhood caused him to question what he believed and what values and ideals he wanted to pass on to his children.

Living in Greenwich Village, Paul and Timmie started a joint search for meaning: leftist politics, self-worship, or religion? All his life, Paul had known good, solid, dependable Christians. However, in the Catholic Church, he met people who were not only good, but also holy. In 1977, Paul published the book *Psychology as Religion: The Cult of Self-Worship*. Paul and Timmie have remained faithful Catholics for decades, raising their six children, now adults, in the Catholic faith.

1. Why should the Romans help Phoebe? Romans 16:1–2

2. What can you learn about Prisca (Priscilla) and Aquila from Acts 18:1–3?

Where is their hometown?	
Where did they have to flee to?	
What is their relationship to one another?	
Where is their occupation?	
Where are they living now?	

3. List three things you learn about Prisca and Aquila from Romans 16:3–5.

Relationship with Paul?	
What they did for Paul?	
What happens in their home?	

4. Who was the first convert for Christ in Asia? Romans 16:5b

5. Identify all the people that Paul names as "kinsmen" in Romans 16.

6. Who might Rufus be? Romans 16:13, Mark 15:21

7. What gesture do Christians show in these verses?

Romans 16:16
1 Thessalonians 5:26
1 Peter 5:14

* How do you greet fellow Christians?

8. What does Paul caution against in Romans 16:17–18?

9. Define the follow dissensions from CCC 2089.

Incredulity
Heresy
Apostasy
Schism

10. Would Galatians 1:8 be a good verse for a Mormon or Jehovah's Witness?

11. How do heretics deceive others? Romans 16:18

12. How should you become wise?

Proverbs 1:7
Proverbs 3:5–8
Matthew 10:16
Romans 16:19

13. What will God do? Romans 16:20

14. What does Paul pray for the believers? Romans 16:20b

" How would you like fellow believers to pray for you?

15. What was kept secret for long ages? Romans 16:25

16. How is the truth made known? Romans 16:25–26

17. What has God commanded and is Paul's overall goal? Romans 16:26b

18. How and where is the mystery made known today? CCC 1204

19. What is the missionary mandate for the laity?

Matthew 28:19–20
CCC 849

* List three (3) practical ways in which you can share the Good News. Then do it!

20. Memorize and share your favorite verse from Romans.

Kerygma

What exactly is the *kerygma*—"the preaching of the Gospel" or "the proclamation of the Good News"—of which Paul speaks? The Greek word *kerygma* appears nine times in the New Testament—three times in the gospels (Matthew 12:41, Mark 16:20, and Luke 11:32), and six times in the Pauline letters (Romans 16:25; 1 Corinthians 1:21, 2:4, 15:14; 2 Timothy 4:17; and Titus 1:3). Sometimes kerygma is translated simply as preaching, proclamation, gospel, or good news. What is the good news that all Christians are called to proclaim?

Kerygma—the heart of the gospel; the core message of Christian faith that all believers are called to proclaim; the initial ardent proclamation by which a person is overwhelmed and brought to the decision to entrust himself to Jesus Christ by faith.

> Proclamation is the permanent priority of mission. The Church cannot elude Christ's explicit mandate, nor deprive men and women of the "Good News" about their being loved and saved by God. "Evangelization will always contain—as the foundation, center, and at the same time the summit of its dynamism—a clear proclamation that, in Jesus Christ . . . salvation is offered to all people, as a gift of God's grace and mercy." All forms of missionary activity are directed to this proclamation, which reveals and gives access to the mystery hidden for ages and made known in Christ (cf. Ephesians 3:3–9; Colossians 1:25–29), the mystery which lies at the heart of the Church's mission and life, as the hinge on which all evangelization turns.
>
> In the complex reality of mission, initial proclamation has a central and irreplaceable role, since it introduces man "into the mystery of the love of God, who invites him to enter into a personal relationship with himself in Christ" and opens the way to conversion. Faith is born of preaching, and every ecclesial community draws its origin and life from the personal response of each believer to that preaching. Just as the whole economy of salvation has its center in Christ, so too all missionary activity is directed to the proclamation of his mystery.
>
> The subject of proclamation is Christ who was crucified, died, and is risen: through him is accomplished our full and authentic liberation from evil, sin and death; through him God bestows "new life" that is divine and eternal. This is the "Good News" which changes man and his history, and which all peoples have a right to hear.
>
> Pope (Saint) John Paul II, *Redemptoris Missio*, December 7, 1990, 44.1

Since you understand the *kerygma*—the Good News of salvation through Jesus Christ—and you have been commissioned and mandated to proclaim the gospel to others, how and when can you do this? By God's grace, will you have the courage to share this pearl of great price?

Monthly Social Activity

This month, your small group will meet for coffee, tea, or a simple breakfast, lunch, or dessert in someone's home. Pray for this social event and for the host or hostess. Try, if at all possible, to attend.

Paul met Jesus on the road to Damascus and was totally transformed. The people Paul mentions in Romans each have a conversion story. How has your Catholic faith transformed your life? What would you tell someone about the source of your faith, hope, and joy? Can you share the story of your faith in three to five minutes?

Some examples:

✤ *I grew up in a Christian home, and always loved the Lord. In adulthood, I just made my childhood faith more mature and sought ways of serving God in my parish as a catechist.*

✤ *While in college, I got in with a bad crowd. Partying became my usual activity. When I hit the bottom of my barrel, I realized that alcohol was robbing me of my joy. So, I went to AA and asked God for help in maintaining sobriety.*

✤ *When my marriage fell apart, I felt lost. It was only in returning to the Catholic Church that I found the love and acceptance that I had always sought.*

CHAPTER 17

Blessings in Christ
Ephesians 1

He destined us in love to be his sons through Jesus Christ,
according to the purpose of his will,
to the praise of his glorious grace
which he freely bestowed on us in the Beloved.
Ephesians 1:5–6

Faith in Jesus Christ brings profound spiritual blessings. The Letter of Paul to the Ephesians was probably written while he was imprisoned in Rome, around AD 60–63. Ephesians, Philippians, Colossians, and Philemon are called the Prison Epistles, since they were all presumably written while he was incarcerated. The Acts of the Apostles reports Paul visiting the city of Ephesus twice. On his first visit, during his second missionary journey, Paul preaches in the synagogue to the Jews. When Paul next visits Ephesus on his third missionary journey, he spends about two years with the Christian community there. At one point, Paul confronts the idol worship of the false goddess Artemis, enraging Demetrius, a silversmith who made his living making silver shrines of Artemis (Acts 19:23ff); this confrontation causes a riot.

Obviously, Paul made many friends and acquaintances in Ephesus, but curiously offers no personal greetings to any of them by name in this letter. This lack of special individual messages in Ephesians leads some to believe that Paul intended this as a circular letter, to be passed from one Christian community to another. The letter is addressed *to the saints who are also faithful in Christ Jesus* (Ephesians 1:1b). These are not saints or holy ones due to their heroic virtue, but on the basis of being made holy and sanctified by Christ in the sacrament of Baptism.

The Letter to the Ephesians divides neatly into two clear segments. The first half (Ephesians 1–3) contains the dogmatic or kerygmatic portion, proclaiming the gospel of salvation in Jesus Christ. The second half (Ephesians 4–6) provides ethical, didactic, parenetic, or moral imperatives, teaching believers how to act and behave. God desires unity and the reconciliation of all creation through Christ and His Church. Individuals can be reconciled to God the Father, thanks to the sacrifice of Jesus Christ on the cross and in union with Him.

The absolute supremacy of Our Lord Jesus Christ emerges from the very beginning of this missive. "Christ" means "Messiah." References to *Christ Jesus, our Lord Jesus Christ, Jesus,* or *Christ* appear eleven times in the first twenty verses of this short epistle. Our Lord Jesus Christ, who suffered, died, and rose from the dead for the salvation of sinful humanity, provides the one hope for sinners' reconciliation with God the Father. Jesus Christ is our sure hope of redemption. Jesus is the provision of God the Father to atone for the sins of Adam and Eve and all of their sinful descendants throughout the ages. The work and the Name of Jesus are powerful and redemptive. *God has highly exalted him and bestowed on him the name which is above every name* (Philippians 2:9).

The Blessed Trinity—God the Father, Jesus Christ, and the Holy Spirit—one God in three Divine Persons, revealed at the Baptism of Jesus in the Jordan (Mark 1:9–11), and again at the Transfiguration (Matthew 17:1ff), emerges here, as well. This central truth of the Christian faith reveals a mystery that can only be believed on faith, with the grace given by God. The word "Trinity" does not appear anywhere in the Bible. But the truth of the doctrine of the Trinity is evident from Genesis to Revelation. Catholics demonstrate belief in the Blessed Trinity when they make the Sign of the Cross and when they profess the Nicene Creed at every Sunday Mass.

God the Father—*Blessed be the God and Father of our Lord Jesus Christ, who*
has blessed us in Christ with every spiritual blessing in the heavenly places,
even as he chose us in him before the foundation of the world,
that we should be holy and blameless before him.
He destined us in love to be his sons through Jesus Christ (Ephesians 1:3–5).

Jesus Christ—*In him [Jesus Christ] we have redemption through his blood,*
the forgiveness of our trespasses according to the riches of his grace
which he lavished upon us (Ephesians 1:7–8).

The Holy Spirit—*In him [Jesus Christ] you also, who have heard the word of truth,*
the gospel of your salvation, and have believed in him [Jesus Christ],
were sealed with the promised Holy Spirit,
who is the guarantee of our inheritance until we acquire the possession of it,
to the praise of his glory (Ephesians 1:13–14).

Christians are baptized "in the name of the Father and of the Son and of the Holy Spirit." Before receiving the sacrament, they respond to a three-part question when asked to confess the Father, the Son, and the Spirit: "I do." "The faith of all Christians rests on the Trinity."   CCC 232

The Trinity is a mystery of faith in the strict sense, one of the "mysteries that are hidden in God, which can never be known unless they are revealed by God." To be sure, God has left traces of his Trinitarian being in his work of creation and in his Revelation throughout the Old Testament. But his inmost Being as Holy Trinity is a mystery that is inaccessible to reason alone or even to Israel's faith before the Incarnation of God's Son and the sending of the Holy Spirit.   CCC 237

God has freely chosen us in love to be his adopted children through faith in Jesus Christ, the Beloved Son of God (Ephesians 1:5 6). This amazing privilege of becoming a child of God, an adopted son or daughter of God the Father, is almost unimaginable. *See what love the*

Father has given us, that we should be called children of God, and so we are. . . . Beloved, we are God's children now; it does not yet appear what we shall be, but we know that when he appears we shall be like him, for we shall see him as he is (1 John 3:1, 3). What does it mean to be an adopted child of God? How could we become like God? Could we become partakers of the divine nature (2 Peter 1:4)? Could anything be more astounding?

Deification—the "formula of exchange"—the eternal Son of God became what we are so that we could become what he is.

Irenaeus—For it was for this end that the Word of God was made man, and he who was the Son of God became the Son of man, that man, having been taken into the Word, and receiving the adoption, might become the son of God.

Gregory of Nyssa—the Word became incarnate so that by becoming as we are, he might make us as he is.

Ephrem the Syrian—He gave us divinity, we gave him humanity.

Daniel A. Keating, *Deification and Grace,*
(Naples, FL: Sapientia Press, 2007), 11–13

Many people today struggle with feelings of inferiority. These can originate in the family of origin and be reinforced later by teachers, media, and advertising. Children may be compared to siblings who are brighter, cuter, more athletic, or more musically inclined. Even adults might feel that others are more successful, more physically fit, better dressed, more accomplished and interesting. And yet, meditating on God's Word reveals that God has blessed each of us, chosen us, loved us, saved us, and adopted us to become sons and daughters of the King of Kings! What could be better than the hope of our inheritance sealed with the promise of the Holy Spirit until we acquire possession of it (Ephesians 1:13–14)?

God's Divine Plan—*For he has made known to us in all wisdom and insight the mystery of his will, according to his purpose which he set forth in Christ as a plan for the fullness of time, to unite all things in him, things in heaven and things on earth* (Ephesians 1:10). In the fullness of time, God plans to bring together the entire cosmos under the Lordship of Jesus Christ. At the end of time, Jesus will be all in all. He will reign supreme over the heavens and the earth.

Sometimes, it can be easy to be caught up in the here and now. Commuting, working, doing mundane chores—shopping, cooking, cleaning, laundry, civic responsibilities, and service commitments—can sap time and energy. Step back and evaluate what significance these activities will have in the eternal perspective. The Morning Offering can present all of our efforts, joys, and sufferings for the glory of God. Remember God's ultimate plan for us, our everlasting hope.

"Blessed be the God and Father of our Lord Jesus Christ, who has blessed us in Christ with every spiritual blessing in the heavenly places" (Eph 1:3). These words of the *Letter to the Ephesians* reveal the eternal design of God the Father, his plan of man's salvation in Christ. It is a universal plan, which concerns all men and women created in the image and likeness of God (cf. Gen 1:26). Just as all are included in the creative work of God "in the beginning," so all are eternally included in the divine plan of salvation, which is to be completely revealed, in the "fullness of time," with the final coming of Christ. In fact, the God who is the "Father of our Lord Jesus Christ . . . chose us in him before the foundation of the world, that we should be holy and blameless before him. He destined us in love to be his sons through Jesus Christ, according to the purpose of his will, to the praise of his glorious grace, which he freely bestowed on us in *the Beloved*. In him we have redemption through his blood, the forgiveness of our trespasses, according to the riches of his grace" (Eph 1:4–7)

The divine plan of salvation—which was fully revealed to us with the coming of Christ—is eternal. . . . It is eternally linked to Christ. It includes everyone.

Pope (Saint) John Paul II, *Redemptoris Mater* (March 25, 1987), 7.1, 2

Paul prays that God will grant believers wisdom and knowledge to comprehend the hope to which Christians have been called. He prays for enlightenment and understanding of the glorious inheritance promised by the Holy Spirit. The power of God to conquer sin and death, Jesus' Resurrection from the dead, is a power beyond human comprehension. And now Jesus sits at the right hand of the Father in the heavens with authority to judge the living and the dead. These are universal truths of the Christian faith. Those who believe and accept them are blessed.

While in the military, Muhammed, a young Shiite Muslim from Bagdad, shared a tent with Massoud, a Christian. Muhammed intended to convert his bunkmate to Islam and asked if Christians had a holy book, like the Qur'an. He was surprised to learn that Christians have a Bible. When he requested a Bible, he was refused; it is a capital crime for Christians to evangelize in Iraq. Massoud suggested that he read the Qur'an very carefully. Ultimately, Muhammed became disillusioned with Islam and intrigued by the person of Jesus. He was discovered reading the Bible, disowned by his family, imprisoned, and ultimately shot by his uncle. But he survived and, after years of waiting, was able to be baptized and escape to France, to live his Catholic faith with his wife and children. *The Price to Pay* by Joseph Fadelle tells the amazing story of the incredible blessings that this Christian now enjoys.

1. How does the Letter of Paul to the Ephesians begin? Ephesians 1:1–3

2. Who chose you? When? Why? For what purpose were you chosen?

Ephesians 1:3–4
CCC 380
CCC 381

* How does the above truth change the way you feel about yourself?

3. Describe one who was created blameless in a special way before time. CCC 492

4. How, why, and for what purpose has God destined us? Ephesians 1:5–6

Ephesians 1:5a   *He destined us in . . .*
Ephesians 1:5b   *to be his . . .*
Ephesians 1:6

5. What does Saint Irenaeus reveal is the glory of God? CCC 294

6. What has Jesus done for us, and why?

Ephesians 1:7–8
CCC 517
CCC 2839

7. Explain the mystery and the purpose in Ephesians 1:9–10.

Ephesians 1:9–10
CCC 1066
CCC 2807

8. With what promise were you sealed?

Ephesians 1:13–14
CCC 1274

* When did you first clearly hear and *understand* the word of truth, the gospel?

9. Who is the guarantee of your inheritance?

Ephesians 1:14
CCC 1107

10. Why and how does Paul pray for the people?

Ephesians 1:15
Ephesians 1:16
Ephesians 1:17

11. What can you learn from these passages?

Deuteronomy 33:1–3
Ephesians 1:17–18

12. How does one come to know God better? Ephesians 1:18

Ephesians 1:18
CCC 158 — _____ seeks _____
CCC 158 *Saint Augustine*

13. What three things do you need to know?

Ephesians 1:18a
Ephesians 1:18b
Ephesians 1:19

14. What can you learn from the following passages?

Psalm 110:1–3
Ephesians 1:20
CCC 668

15. Where can you find Christ today? CCC 669

16. In the Apostles' Creed and the Nicene Creed, where is Jesus found after His Resurrection from the dead? CCC Part One, The Credo, after CCC 184, page 49.
Where does Paul situate Jesus? Ephesians 1:20–21

17. What is the mysterious plan of God and our hope? CCC 425

18. Compare the following verses.

Psalm 8:1–6
Ephesians 1:22
Colossians 1:18–20

* How does contemporary society react to words like "rule," "authority," "power," and "dominion?" What type of rule or authority do you want to be under?

19. What can you learn from these verses?

Romans 12:4–5
Ephesians 1:22–23
Colossians 2:17
CCC 830

20. Describe the saints who are faithful in Christ Jesus. Ephesians 1:1, CCC 1213

* Have you known any saints? How could you become one?

Monthly Social Activity

This month, your small group will meet for coffee, tea, or a simple breakfast, lunch, or dessert in someone's home. Pray for this social event and for the host or hostess. Try, if at all possible, to attend.

Think about examples in which you saw God bring about unity in an amazing way.

Some examples:

❦ *After 35 years of marriage, Bob had an affair with another woman. His wife Mary and their adult children were devastated. Mary started to pray for her husband, despite her pain. When their daughter married, Bob realized his sin at the wedding Mass. He repented to Mary and his children and received mercy.*

❦ *When terrorists stormed a synagogue and killed people at worship, the rabbi in our town open the doors to the synagogue so that people of all denominations could pray together for an end to hatred and violence.*

❦ *People from several churches in our town committed to praying together for an end to abortion, in front of the abortion clinic close to our town.*

CHAPTER 18

Death to Life
Ephesians 2

For by grace you have been saved through faith;
and this is not your own doing,
it is the gift of God—
not because of works, lest any man should boast.
Ephesians 2:8–9

Jesus brings sinners back from spiritual death to life. Sin is deadly. Temptations to sin can appear to be appealing. But, after succumbing to the temptation to disobey God, the consequences bring guilt and shame to a healthy conscience. The forbidden fruit tastes bitter in the end. What looked so enticing becomes oppressive. If you have never encountered this phenomenon, ask someone who is struggling to deal with an addiction what he or she is experiencing. The consequences of sin can also affect not only the guilty person, but innocent loved ones as well. Stories of pain and suffering abound, as part of the condition of fallen humanity.

No one deserves salvation. No one can earn salvation. What do you have to barter with God that He has not given you? Grace is the free gift of God to needy souls. God gives sinners the grace to repent and believe in His mercy. Christians are mindful of being needy sinners who have been saved by God's gift of grace. A Christian is one beggar telling another beggar where the bread is. The virtue of humility enables the penitent to realize that: "There but for the grace of God go I."

But God, who is rich in mercy, out of the great love with which he loved us, even when we were dead through our trespasses, made us alive together with Christ (by grace you have been saved), and raised us up with him, and made us sit with him in the heavenly places in Christ Jesus, that in the coming ages he might show the immeasurable riches of his grace in kindness toward us in Christ Jesus (Ephesians 2:4–7). God is rich in mercy. His steadfast love endures forever.

> Let us, therefore, dearly beloved, give thanks to God the Father, through His Son, in the Holy Spirit, who on account of the great mercy with which He has loved us, has been merciful to us; and when we were dead in our sins He made us to live again together in Christ, so that in Him we might be a new creation. . . . O Christian, acknowledge your worth! Having been made a partner of the divine nature, do not return to your old baseness by degenerate conduct. . . . Recall that you have been rescued from the power of darkness and have been transferred into the light and kingdom of God.
>
> Saint Leo the Great (AD 400–461), *Sermons*, 21, 3

For by grace you have been saved through faith; and this is not your own doing, it is the gift of God—not because of works, lest any man should boast (Ephesians 2:8–9). Grace represents the benevolence shown by God to the human race. It is a totally gratuitous gift on which a person has absolutely no claim. Faith is an assent of the mind to what God has revealed. But faith demands more than merely intellectual assent. Demons know that Jesus is God, but it does them no good. Faith begins with the grace to believe in God and all that the Church teaches, and then genuine saving faith requires obedience to the commands of God. Live what you believe.

"For by grace," [Paul] says, "you have been saved." But lest the greatness of the benefits inflate you, see how he brings you down: "By grace you have been saved," he says, "through faith." And then again, lest a violence be done free will, after he has added what pertains to us he takes it away again when he says, "and that not of ourselves." The faith, he means, is not from ourselves; for if He had not come, if He had not called, how should we be able to believe? "For how shall they believe," [Paul] says, "unless they do hear?" Thus the work of faith is not ours. "It is the gift," he says, "of God."

Saint John Chrysostom (AD 344–407),
Homilies on the Epistle to the Ephesians, 4,2

Salvation involves God liberating a sinner from the consequences of sin and evil. Jesus won salvation for the human race by His death on the cross. He promised the repentant thief on the cross that *"Today you will be with me in Paradise"* (Luke 23:43). You *were saved* when Jesus died. A person *is saved* when he or she repents of sin and asks God for mercy. That person *will be saved* when Jesus pronounces the final judgment on that individual soul. Each person will undergo a particular judgment at the hour of death, revealing how well that person cooperated with God's grace. This judgment will be confirmed at the Last Judgment, when Jesus returns in glory to judge the living and the dead (Matthew 25:21–46). Some insist that all you have to do to be saved is to profess faith in Jesus, but this view is not consistent with Scripture, nor does it align with the warnings of Jesus.

Pride and self-sufficiency have no place in the life of a believer. One who claims to be saved, assured of his place and reward in heaven, may be guilty of the sin of presumption. Only God can judge the human soul. Paul confessed that he did not even judge himself. Christians believe in God, and then they run the race. Sometimes believers fall. They repent and avail themselves of the Sacrament of Reconciliation. Then they get up again and continue to run the race, with God's help. Each person has free will. The believer may fall, but refuse to repent, and then stop following Jesus. The spiritual battle continues throughout life. At the end of Ephesians, Paul warns believers to stand against the wiles of the devil (Ephesians 6:11).

Gentiles were once separated from Christ. They were also excluded from the covenant promises to Israel. Those who were once estranged are now brought near by the blood of Jesus, our peace, Who breaks down the walls of hostility. Jesus provides reconciliation with and access to God the Father.

> I give glory to Jesus Christ, the God who has made you wise; for I have observed that you are set in faith unshakeable, as if nailed to the cross of our Lord Jesus Christ in body and in soul; and that you are confirmed in love by the Blood of Christ, firmly believing in regard to our Lord that He is truly of the family of David according to the flesh, and God's Son by the will and power of God, truly born of a Virgin, baptized by John so that all justice might be fulfilled by Him, in the time of Pontius Pilate and Herod the Tetrarch truly nailed in the flesh on our behalf—and we are of the fruit of His divinely blessed passion—so that by means of His Resurrection He might raise aloft a banner for His saints and believers in every age, whether among the Jews or among the Gentiles, united in a single body in His Church.
>
> Saint Ignatius of Antioch (AD † 110), *Letter to the Smyrnaeans*, 1,1

Strangers and sojourners—are those people who do not belong in the group. Many people experience a feeling of not belonging on the first day in a new school or in moving to a new place. Children from dysfunctional homes may find it difficult to experience acceptance and a sense of belonging anywhere. People with disabilities often face challenges in new and unfamiliar situations. Immigrants and newcomers can be met with suspicion, rather than welcome. So most people can understand what the Gentiles must have felt like in the First Century.

> The Gentiles were transformed once they had embraced the faith. With the richness of the salvation wrought by Christ, the walls separating the different cultures collapsed. God's promise in Christ now became a universal offer. . . . From their different locations and traditions all are called in Christ to share in the unity of the family of God's children. It is Christ who enables the two peoples to become "one." Those who were "far off" have come "near," thanks to the newness brought by the Paschal Mystery. Jesus destroys the walls of division and creates unity in a new and unsurpassed way through our sharing in his mystery. This unity is so deep that the Church can say with Saint Paul: "You are no longer strangers and sojourners, but you are saints and members of the household of God" (Ephesians 2:19).
>
> Pope (Saint) John Paul II, *Fides et Ratio*, September 14, 1998, 70.2

Who will minister to the strangers and sojourners? Who helps those who feel left out, abandoned, or unwanted? The Catholic Church accepts everyone. If you go to a Catholic Mass anywhere in the world, you will see the elderly and the young. You will hear babies crying and see children trying to sit still. You will see people with disabilities, people in wheelchairs and walkers. Anyone can follow when to kneel and when to stand. Even if you cannot understand the language in which the Mass is being said, you can pray the Lord's Prayer and the Sanctus in your heart and in your own language. Whether you are rich or poor, young or old, man or woman, black, white, red, or yellow, you will be invited to receive the Body, Blood, Soul and Divinity of Our Lord Jesus Christ in the Eucharist, if you are baptized and in the state of grace. You can receive the greatest treasure on earth for free!

James Joyce, an American writer of the last century, described the Catholic Church: "Here comes everyone!" Jesus established a Church on earth to help everyone experience the love and mercy of God. Saint Paul affirms this truth. *So then you are no longer strangers and sojourners, but you are fellow citizens with the saints and members of the household of God, built upon the foundation of the apostles and prophets, Christ Jesus himself being the cornerstone, in whom the whole structure is joined together and grows into a holy temple in the Lord; in whom you also are built into it for a dwelling place of God in the Spirit* (Ephesians 2:19–22).

Ronda Chervin and her twin sister were perhaps the most alienated little children living in New York City. Born of unmarried parents who met in the Communist Party, they were of Jewish ancestry, but being raised as atheists. They simply did not fit in with any of the children in their neighborhood or school. The Jewish children shunned them because they were not observant Jews. The Catholic children avoided them because they could not even understand what atheists were.

When the twins were eight years old, their parents (still unmarried) separated for good, which was devastating to the children. They were sent for awhile to stay at the summer cottage of a Christian grandmother, alone, and in a new place.

Later, Ronda was studying philosophy at the University of Rochester, when she returned home for Thanksgiving vacation. She noticed her mother watching "The Catholic Hour" on television, featuring two Catholic philosophers, Dietrich von Hildebrand and his fiancé Alice Jourdain. They were discussing truth and love. After meeting them, Ronda decided to transfer to Fordham University.

Unexpectedly, a scholarship emerged for Ronda to go on a Catholic art tour of Europe with her Fordham professors (who probably provided the scholarship as a means to facilitate her conversion to Christ). At Chartres Cathedral, Ronda was stunned by the magnificence and began to cry as she encountered beauty and truth.

At the age of twenty-one, Ronda was baptized and later helped to lead her twin sister, her mother, and her husband into the Catholic Church. In the Catholic Church, Ronda found and experienced the sense of belonging that had evaded her as a child. Ronda Chervin earned a PhD in philosophy from Fordham University and is the author of more than sixty books

1. Explain where believers were in the past. Ephesians 2:1–2

2. What are the passions of the flesh?

Ephesians 2:3
CCC 2515

3. Explain "justification."

Romans 4:22–25
Ephesians 2:4–5
CCC 654

4. What characteristic of God emerges here?

Ephesians 2:4a
CCC 211

5. When and where can you experience God's love?

Ephesians 2: 4b
CCC 1073

6. When and how does God save sinners? Ephesians 2:5

7. Find the treasure in these passages.

Ephesians 2:6–7
CCC 1003
CCC 2796

* When are you earthly troubled, and when are you heavenly minded?

8. How were you saved? Ephesians 2:8–9

9. Who are believers and what should they do? Ephesians 2:10

10. Fill in the blanks from Ephesians 2:12.

   Remember that you were at that time _____ from _____,

   alienated from the commonwealth of Israel, and _____ to the covenants of

   _____, having no _____, and _____ _____ in the world.

11. How is a sinner brought into the body? Ephesians 2:13

12. Where can a sinner find peace?

Ephesians 2:14
CCC 2305

13. By what means is one reconciled to God?

Ephesians 2:16
CCC 616

* What do you think of when you see a cross or a crucifix?

14. Can you find fulfillment in these verses?

Isaiah 57:18–19
Ephesians 2:17

* When have you been far away from God? How have you been brought near?

15. Through whom can you gain access to God the Father? Ephesians 2:18

16. Fill in the blanks from Ephesians 2:19.

So then you are no longer _____ and _____, but you

are fellow citizens with the saints and members of the _____ of _____

* Recall a time when you felt left out. Where do feel a sense of belonging?

17. What is the foundation of the Catholic Church?

Ephesians 2:20
CCC 857

18. What structure should believers grow into and become?

Ephesians 2:21
CCC 756

19. How is this made possible? CCC 797

20. What can you become? Ephesians 2:22

CHAPTER 19

Ministry to Gentiles
Ephesians 3

For this reason I bow my knees before the Father,
from whom every family in heaven and on earth is named,
that according to the riches of his glory
he may grant you to be strengthened with might
through his Spirit in the inner man,
and that Christ may dwell in your hearts through love.
Ephesians 3:14–17

Paul ministers to the Gentiles. Here, Paul identifies himself as a prisoner for Christ on behalf of *you* Gentiles, leading one to believe that Paul is writing especially to the Gentile Christians living in Ephesus and elsewhere. God's grace was given to Paul in order to perform a specific ministry of evangelism and discipleship for a particular group of people. God revealed his mystery in Christ for Paul to share with those outside of the nation of Israel. What does this mystery encompass?

In the Symbol of the faith the Church confesses the mystery of the Holy Trinity and of the plan of God's "good pleasure" for all creation: the Father accomplishes the "mystery of his will" by giving his beloved Son and his Holy Spirit for the salvation of the world and for the glory of his name. Such is the mystery of Christ, revealed and fulfilled in history according to the wisely ordered plan that St. Paul calls the "plan of the mystery" and the patristic tradition will call the "economy of the Word incarnate" or the "economy of salvation."   CCC 1066

The mystery encompasses the divine plan of salvation that God revealed through the life, teaching, passion, death, and Resurrection of Jesus Christ, his only begotten Son. Jesus Christ, true God and true man, reconciled sinful humanity to God the Father. The Holy Spirit revealed this mystery to the holy apostles and prophets. When Paul uses the word "holy" to describe apostles, he means that they have been "set apart for God" or sanctified by virtue of baptism. The apostles have seen the mystery unfold as they observed the life, teachings, and ministry of Jesus. Now these apostles share the mystery of salvation through Jesus Christ with others.

Paul indicates that Gentiles now enjoy special new privileges. Gentiles are now joint heirs of God's benevolence with their Jewish brothers and sisters. Jews and Gentiles together become members of the one body of Christ in His Church. Gentiles are now beneficiaries of the promises that God made to Abraham, by virtue of their relationship with Jesus through accepting the gospel.

> That which in other ages was not known has now been clearly shown and has now been revealed to the sons of men. Indeed, there was always a natural manifestation of the one almighty God, among all right thinking men; and the majority, who had not entirely divested themselves of shame in the presence of the truth, apprehended the eternal beneficence through divine providence. . . . The Father and Creator of all things, therefore, is apprehended by all by means of an innate power and without instruction, in a manner suitable to all. . . . Nor is it possible for any race to live anywhere, whether they be tillers of the soil or nomads, nor even be they city-dwellers, without being imbued with faith in a Higher Being.
>
> Saint Clement of Alexandria (AD 150–216), *Stromateis*, 5, 13, 87, 1

Any rational, thinking person can reason that *Someone* created this universe, and *Someone* created human life. Most people wonder about God, life, death, judgment, heaven, and hell. What happens when this life ends? Is there something more that awaits people after death? Who will judge the deeds of one's life, for good or evil? These questions received answers in the person of Jesus of Nazareth. Our Lord not only achieved salvation for sinners, Jesus conquered sin and death. Jesus returned from the grave to prove that there is hope beyond this life. God's previously hidden plan for salvation has now been revealed in Jesus Christ.

> Believe first of all that God is one, that He created all things and set them in order, and brought out of non-existence everything that is, and that He contains all things while He Himself in uncontained.
>
> Hermes (AD 140), *The Shepherd-Mandates*, 1, 1

The first leap of faith for an atheist requires considering that God exists and that there is one God and Creator of all things. To imagine that God made all things out of nothing requires an infusion of grace along with Divine Revelation. Humans cannot see the air we breathe, but we can visualize the power of air and wind in a hurricane or tornado. Similarly, we cannot see God, but we see His power in truth, goodness, and beauty. The magnificent works of God spring up everywhere.

Once one accepts that there is a God, the soil is prepared to next consider the implications of the supernatural works of God performed by Jesus. Who can walk on water, still a storm, forgive sins, heal the blind, and raise the dead to life? Only God. Jesus did all those things. Jesus is God. No one else can do these things. No one walks on water, quiets storms, and raises the dead, apart from the power of God. Miracles can only be done by Jesus or through the power of His Name.

The unsearchable riches of Christ are precious jewels of great price that no one could obtain apart from Jesus. Who else can forgive sins? Who else can reconcile a repentant sinner to God the Father? Who can control the forces of nature, heal diseases, and raise the dead? Who can make us adopted sons of God the Father? Only Jesus can do these things. Because of our faith in Jesus, we have boldness and confidence in approaching God the Father with our prayers and requests.

Paul prays for the believers. Bowing his knees before God the Father, Paul offers a spectacular prayer. Paul asks for every spiritual gift to be given to Christians. These are gifts that Christians today desire, as well.

Paul's Prayer to God the Father
Ephesians 3:14–19

For this reason I bow my knees before the Father,
> *from whom every family in heaven and on earth is named,*
> *that according to the riches of his glory*
> *he may grant you*
>> *to be strengthened with might through his Spirit in the inner man,*
>> *and that Christ may dwell in your hearts through faith;*
>> *that you, being rooted and grounded in love,*
>> *may have power to comprehend with all the saints*
>>> *what is the breadth and length and height and depth,*
>> *and to know the love of Christ which surpasses knowledge,*
>> *that you may be filled with all the fullness of God.*

The unsearchable, unfathomable, boundless riches of Christ can be seen in His humble birth as a baby, in poverty, in Bethlehem, to become one of us, and in His horrific death like a criminal on the cross to atone for our sins and redeem us. The amazing gift of the Eucharist completes Paul's prayer because in Holy Communion, Jesus does dwell in us. Believers experience the love of Christ and the presence of Our Lord in our midst throughout the ages. The Holy Spirit dwells in the inner man. This truth enabled the apostles to have the courage to suffer martyrdom.

In the name of Christ's Resurrection the Church serves the life that comes from God himself, in close union with and humble service to the Spirit. . . . United with the Spirit, the Church is supremely aware of the reality of *the inner man*, of what is deepest and most essential in man, *because it is spiritual and incorruptible.* At this level the Spirit grafts the "root of immortality," from which the new life springs. This is man's life in God, which, as a fruit of God's salvific self-communication in the Holy Spirit, can develop and flourish only by the Spirit's action. Therefore Saint Paul speaks to God on behalf of believers, to whom he declares, "I bow my knees before the Father . . . , that he may grant you . . . to be strengthened with might through his Spirit in the inner man."

Pope (Saint) John Paul II, *Dominum et Vivificantem,* May 18, 1986, 58.1–2

Paul's prayer dovetails with a prayer that Catholics hear the priest pray at every Holy Mass as he prepares the gifts of bread and wine: "May we come to share in the divinity of Christ, who humbled Himself to share in our humanity." The ultimate goal of Christians is to become Christ-like, and to one day behold Him, face to face, in the Beatific Vision. Jesus became man so that we might share in His divine nature—partake of His divinity. This amazing transfer is called deification or divination. Jesus takes on our humanity and offers us divinity. No human being can accomplish this process alone; it can only occur with divine intervention.

Doxology—Paul ends his prayer by revealing the source of supernatural power in a hymn of praise to God. *Now to him who by the power at work within us is able to do far more abundantly than all that we ask or think, to him be glory in the Church and in Christ Jesus to all generations, for ever and ever. Amen* (Ephesians 3:20–21). God can do even more that we can ask or imagine. So let us boldly ask.

Holly Ordway grew up in a secular, nonreligious family. Nobody ever went to church, and they had no Bible in the house. Her family did have a nativity set at Christmas, which she played with, by moving the sheep closer to Baby Jesus. But she didn't know what it represented, and no one ever explained it to her. The result was that she knew nothing whatsoever about Christianity. She wasn't hostile to the faith, just uninformed. When a classmate in school asked if she believed in God, she replied, "I don't know. Maybe God's real, maybe not." The boy announced that then she was an agnostic, and she was happy to learn a new vocabulary word.

As a teenager, Holly became concerned with questions of right and wrong, and she developed a longing for meaning and connection. Being a very bookish girl, she read C. S. Lewis's *Chronicles of Narnia* and J. R. R. Tolkien's *Lord of the Rings*, which became the creative work that most shaped her life. God's grace was beginning to work in her imagination.

In college, Holly believed that religion was an historical curiosity and that everything could be explained by science. Holly felt that it was important for her to be a good person, but as an atheist, she could not explain a reason for this. Despite her materialistic worldview, as a doctoral student of English literature, she chose to study J. R. R. Tolkien and read John Donne and other Catholic poets.

After having her imagination stirred by Catholic writers, Holly received the grace to investigate the claims of Christianity by reading the gospels. She came to realize the truth of the Resurrection of Jesus. Later, she came to realize that the Church is not merely a human organization, but truly is the body of Christ, animated by His Spirit. Holly wrote in her memoir, *Not God's Type*, that becoming a Catholic was by far the best thing she's ever done and the most significant event of her life. Holly now embraces the graces of her Catholic faith with joy and gratitude.

The Knowledge of the Mystery Hidden in Christ

Though saints have uncovered many mysteries and wonders, and devout souls have understood them in this earthly condition of ours, yet the greater part still remains to be revealed and understood in the world to come.

Why is there a crucifix in every Catholic Church? Christ is Risen! He lives! Why is Jesus portrayed in His suffering? Is this not the greatest manifestation of His love? In contemporary culture, love is illustrated in hearts. Many Catholics meditate on the Sacred Heart of Jesus and the Immaculate Heart of Mary, as well as the Divine Mercy image. God loved us and emptied Himself for our salvation.

For this reason the apostle Paul said of Christ: *In him are hidden all the treasure of the wisdom and knowledge of God.* The soul cannot enter into these treasures, nor attain them, unless it first experiences the taste of suffering, enduring interior and exterior labors, and unless it first receives from God blessings in the intellect and in the senses, and has undergone spiritual training.

The highest wisdom attainable in this life encompasses the love and sacrifice offered to sinful human beings by a perfectly good and loving God.

Christians learn that it is quite impossible to reach the riches and wisdom of God except by first entering the thicket of suffering, in such a way that the soul finds there its consolation and desire. The soul that longs for divine wisdom chooses first, and in truth, to participate in Jesus' suffering of the cross.

Saint Paul therefore urges the Ephesians *not to grow weary in the midst of tribulations,* but to be *rooted and grounded in love, so that they may know with all the saints the breadth, the length, the heights and the depth—to know what is beyond knowledge, the love of Christ, so as to be filled with all the fullness of God.*

The gate that gives entry into these riches of his wisdom is the cross; because it is a narrow gate, while many seek the joys that can be gained through wisdom, it is given to few to desire to pass through suffering.

Let us rejoice, Beloved,
and let us go forth to behold ourselves in your beauty,
to the mountain and to the hill,
to where the pure water flows, and further, deep into the thicket.

Saint John of the Cross, (AD 1542–1591),
The Spiritual Canticle, 36.

Kavanaugh, Kieran, OCD, *The Collected Works of St. John of the Cross,*
(Washington, DC: ICS Publications, 2017)

1. How does Paul identify himself in Ephesians 3:1–3?

2. What is the mystery of which Paul speaks?

Ephesians 3:3–6
Colossians 1:26–27

3. How was Paul made an apostle? Ephesians 3:7

4. What does grace enable?

Ephesians 3:8
CCC 424

5. Discover God's innermost secret.

1 John 4:8, 16
Ephesians 3:9–10
CCC 221

6. What mystery can you participate in?

Ephesians 3:9–11
CCC 772
CCC 773

* How would you describe "union with God?"

** What does holiness look like? How can one achieve holiness?

7. By what means can you find confidence of access to God?

Ephesians 3:11–12
CCC 2778

8. What does Paul ask of the believers in Ephesians 3:13?

*** Have you ever "lost heart?" When?

9. For what purpose does Paul offer his suffering? Ephesians 3:13

10. What prayer posture does Paul take in Ephesians 3:14?

* When do you bow or kneel before the Father?

11. What two things can you say about God the Father?

CCC 239
CCC 239

** Do you more often think of God's authority or His goodness and loving care?

12. What can you learn about natural human fatherhood?

Ephesians 3:15
CCC 2214

* Who is your favorite father figure in literature or movies?

** Who has been a good father or father figure for you?

13. What special privilege does God give to married couples? CCC 2367

14. How can you be strengthened in your inner person?

Ephesians 3:16
CCC 2713
CCC 2714

15. What does Paul pray in Ephesians 3:17a?

16. What is prayer in the New Covenant?

Ephesians 3:18–21
CCC 2565

17. How should Christians pray? CCC 2641

18. How does Paul end his prayer in Ephesians 3:20–21?

19. Fill in the blanks from Paul's Prayer in Ephesians 3:14–19.

For this reason I _____ my _____ before the _____,

from whom every _____ in _____ and in _____ is named,

that according to the _____ of _____ _____ he may grant you to

be _____ with _____ through his _____ in the

_____ _____, and that _____ may dwell in your

_____ through _____;

that you, being rooted and grounded in _____, may have _____

to _____ with all the _____ what is the breadth and

_____ and _____ and _____, and to know the

_____ of _____ which surpasses _____, that

you may be _____ with all the _____ of _____.

20. God is able to do more than we ask, so write a prayer of intercession to God.

CHAPTER 20

Unity in Christ
Ephesians 4

*There is one body and one Spirit,
just as you were called to the one hope that belongs to your call,
one Lord, one faith, one baptism, one God and Father of us all,
who is above all and through all and in all.*
Ephesians 4:4–6

God desires unity in the body of Christ. Paul, who suffers imprisonment because of his faith in Jesus, exhorts believers to walk humbly with the Lord, in a manner worthy of their Christian calling. Humility, in ancient times and even today, is not a virtue found in excess. Meekness and humility are not even admired or sought after as virtues in many cultures. Rather, pride, arrogance, narcissism, and ruthlessness seem to be more evident. But Christianity is countercultural. Paul exhorts Christians to be more patient, forbearing with one another, in an effort to maintain peace and unity in the Spirit. There is one body, one Spirit, one hope, one Lord, one faith, one baptism, and one God and Father of us all.

Indeed, this oneness of the Church is indicated in the Songs of Songs, when the Holy Spirit, speaking in the Lord's name, says: "One is my dove, my perfect one, to her mother the only one, the chosen of her that bore her." If someone does not hold fast to this unity of the Church, can he imagine that he still holds the faith? If he resists and withstands the Church, can he still be confident that he is in the Church, when the blessed Apostle Paul teaches this very thing and displays the sacred sign of unity when he says: "One body and one spirit, one hope of your calling, one Lord, one faith, one Baptism, one God?" Most especially must we bishops, who exercise authority in the Church, hold firmly and insist upon this unity, whereby we may demonstrate also that the episcopate itself is one and undivided. Let no one mislead the brotherhood with a lie; let no one corrupt the faith by a faithless perversion of the truth. The episcopate is one, of which each bishop holds his part within the undivided structure. The Church also is one, however widely she has spread among the multitude through her fruitful increase. . . . The Church is bathed in the light of the Lord, and pours her rays over the whole world; but it is one light that is spread everywhere, and the unity of her structure is undivided.
Saint Cyprian of Carthage (†AD 258), The Unity of the Catholic Church, 4

On the night before He died, Jesus prayed to God the Father for the unity of the Church, *"Holy Father, keep them in your name, which you have given me, that they may be one, even as we are one"* (John 17:11). While Jesus and the Apostle Paul prayed for unity and exhorted harmony, there are now more than thirty thousand different denominations, all calling themselves Christians, all believing that they have found the truth and are obeying God's will. How could this be so? How could the unity that Jesus prayed for be so lacking in the world? The Trinity is One, and God expects the Church to mirror the love and unity in the Blessed Trinity.

. . . Let us note that the very tradition, teaching, and faith of the Catholic Church from the beginning, which the Lord gave, was preached by the Apostles, and was preserved by the Fathers. On this was the Church founded; and if anyone departs from this, he neither is nor any longer ought to be called a Christian: there is a Trinity, holy and perfect, acknowledged as God, in Father, Son, and Holy Spirit . . .

It is consistent in Itself, indivisible in nature, and Its activity is one. The Father does all things through the Word in the Holy Spirit; and thus the unity of the Holy Trinity is preserved; and thus there is preached in the Church one God, "who is over all, and through all, and in all." He is *over all* as Father, as beginning, as source; and *through all*, through the Word; and *in all*, in the Holy Spirit.

The Spirit, then, being established in us, the Son and the Father come; and they make their dwelling in us. For the Trinity is indivisible, and its Godhead is one; and there is one God over all and through all and in all. This is the faith of the Catholic Church; for on the Trinity the Lord founded it and rooted it, when He said to His disciples, "Go out and instruct every people, baptizing them in the name of the Father and of the Son and of the Holy Spirit." But if the Spirit were a creature, He would not have joined Himself with the Father, lest the Trinity be dissimilar within Itself, lest It have united in Itself anything strange or foreign. Indeed what could be lacking in God that He should assume any foreign substance, and be glorified with it? Inconceivable!

Saint Athansius (AD 295–373),
Four Letters to Serapion of Thmuis, 1, 28; 3,6

God is one, and He expects His followers to maintain unity and harmony as well. And yet there are divisions in families, rifts in parishes, splits in churches, and animosity in communities. Peace and harmony elude the people of God. What can be done to restore peace and harmony in marriages, families, churches, communities, and the culture? Perhaps prayer would be the best starting point. We get ourselves into these messes, but only God can restore peace and unity.

God gives gifts of ministry to the church. Elsewhere in the Pauline letters there are lists of gifts that God gives to individual believers (Romans 12:6–8; 1 Corinthians 12:4–10). Each individual Christian receives particular gifts for the building up of the church. Here Paul describes a variety of roles that God assigns and equips for the building up of the body of Christ. God anoints specific people in five different positions for the good of everyone—apostles, prophets, evangelists, pastors, and teachers, as gifts to the church. *And his gifts* *were that some should be apostles, some prophets, some evangelists, some pastors and teachers, to equip the saints for the work of ministry, for building up the body of Christ, until we all attain to the unity of faith and of the knowledge of the Son of God, to mature manhood, to the measure of the stature of the fullness of Christ* (Ephesians 4:11–13).

Note that God chooses and assigns people to these roles. Some people might think that they have a *right* to be an evangelist or a pastor. But a vocation is not the same as an occupation. Anyone has the right to study to become an accountant, or a nurse, or a carpenter. But God reserves the exclusive right to call specific people and anoint them for particular ministries. The humble and detached attitude of Saint John Neumann when he was then bishop of Philadelphia illustrates how a servant of God may react to being chosen by God and serving at His pleasure.

> I am prepared without any hesitation to the leave the episcopacy. I have taken this burden out of obedience, and I have labored with all my powers to fulfill the duties of my office, and with God's help, as I hope, not without fruit. . . . I am, indeed, prepared either to remain in the same condition in which I am at present, or if God so inspires His Holiness to give the whole administration of the diocese to the Most Reverend James Wood, I am equally prepared to resign from the episcopate and to go where I may more securely prepare myself for death and for the account which must be rendered to the Divine Justice. I desire nothing but to fulfill the wish of the Holy Father whatever it may be.
> Saint John Neumann (AD 1811–1860), *Letter to Cardinal Barnabo.*

Grow into spiritual maturity. Christians achieve their ultimate goal by following Christ, listening to the promptings of the Holy Spirit, and obeying them. In this way, believers try to imitate Christ, to become Christ-like. *Rather, speaking the truth in love, we are to grow up in every way into him who is the head into Christ, from whom the whole body, joined and knit together by every joint with which it is supplied, when each part is working properly, makes bodily growth and upbuilds itself in love* (Ephesians 4:15–16). It takes courage to walk in God's truth and to speak the truth in love. Christians need to challenge each other to renounce sin and to grow in holiness. Jesus outlines the process by which a believer should confront the sin of an erring brother or sister in Matthew 18:15–17.

Speaking the truth in love becomes difficult in a secular culture of relativism. When people acknowledge objective biblical standards, right and wrong behaviors are clearly explained in the Sacred Scriptures. In a culture that champions individual expression, one person's opinion becomes as good as another's. Truth and love go hand in hand. Christians can unwittingly become harsh and judgmental, pushing people away from the mercy of God. On the other hand, in fear and weakness, expressing charity without orthodoxy can result in insipid sentimentality, depriving people of the impetus to repent and taste God's mercy and love. Objective truth does exist. Sin is sin. Virtue is virtue. Tell the truth in charity.

We are moving toward a dictatorship of relativism, which does not recognize anything as for certain and which has as its highest goal one's own ego and one's own desires. However, we have a different goal: the Son of God, true man. Being an "adult" means having a faith which does not follow the waves of today's fashions or the latest novelties. A faith which is deeply rooted in friendship with Christ is adult and mature. . . . In Christ, truth and love coincide. To the extent that we draw near to Christ, in our own life, truth and love merge. Love without truth would be blind; truth without love would be like "a resounding gong or a clashing cymbal" (1 Corinthians 13:1).   Pope Benedict XVI, *Homily,* April 18, 2005

Paul exhorts believers to abandon their former sinful way of life and to be renewed in the spirit, in the likeness of God in true holiness and righteousness. Even after meeting Christ and experiencing freedom from sin, temptations arise to slip back into old patterns of darkness and wickedness. Christians encourage one another to walk in the light of Christ and to strive for holiness. *Therefore, putting away falsehood, let every one speak the truth with his neighbor, for we are members one of another* (Ephesians 4:25). Anger is a normal human emotion. Jesus displayed righteous anger in dealing with the moneychangers in the Temple. Paul urges believers not to nurse anger, but to douse that anger at the end of the day. Christians must work, not steal, and speak to edify. They must shun bitterness, wrath, and slander, and rather be kind and forgive one another, as God forgives.

John, a physicist, grew up without any faith. When he met Mary, a Catholic, he saw an inner glow, a real goodness, about her. Her uncle was a priest and performed their marriage, even though John was a total unbeliever and had never been baptized. Theirs was not a sacramental marriage. When Mary became pregnant, she reminded John that he had agreed that their children would be raised in the faith. Their children were baptized, and when Mary went to Mass with the children, John tagged along. He wanted to be with his family and desired a sense of unity.

In fact, John's longing for unity led him to attend Sunday Mass with his wife and children for twelve years. Throughout all of these years, Mary never nagged John. Never once did she say, "I wish you were Catholic" or anything like that. And leaving him alone was the best thing she could have done for him.

One Sunday, when his wife and daughters went up to receive Holy Communion, John felt left out. They were getting something (Someone) that he wasn't. John didn't believe yet, but he wanted to believe. Grace was at work. John received a religious experience a week later in which he understood that Catholicism is true. He was baptized and confirmed at the Easter Vigil. John's longing for unity in his marriage and family led him to encounter God's personal love for him.

1. How can one maintain unity of the Spirit?

Ephesians 4:1–3
CCC 2219

2. Explain how the Catholic Church is one, holy, catholic, and apostolic.

Ephesians 4:4–6
CCC 866
CCC 867
CCC 868
CCC 869

3. How can the Church maintain unity with the diversity of cultures?

Ephesians 4:4
CCC 172
CCC 173
CCC 174

* Have you ever celebrated Mass in a different country or language?

4. What have you received? Ephesians 4:7

5. What can you learn from the following passages?

Ephesians 4:8–10
CCC 661
CCC 2795

6. What does God provide for His Church?

Ephesians 4:11–12
CCC 1575
CCC 1576

* Name your pastor and your bishop. Will you pray for them regularly?

** Identify contemporary Catholic evangelists, including lay Catholic evangelists.

7. What is your goal as a Christian? How can you achieve this?

Ephesians 4:13–14
CCC 798
CCC 2045
CCC 2518

* Name one practical way in which you could grow in holiness.

8. How and when should you *speak the truth in love*? Ephesians 4:15

9. In what ways can the Church be built up? Ephesians 4:15–16

10. How do people behave before they meet Christ? Ephesians 4:17–19

11. What brings about positive change in life? Ephesians 4:20–21

12. How can you become spiritually transformed?

Ephesians 4:22
CCC 1473
Ephesians 4:23–24
CCC 1695

13. What should you do for your neighbor? Ephesians 4:25

14. Find three commands in the following verses.

Ephesians 4:26a
Ephesians 4:26b
Ephesians 4:27

* List practical ways you could achieve the commands in Ephesians 4:26–27.

15. What can you give the poor besides money? Ephesians 4:28, CCC 2443–2444

16. How should a good Catholic speak? Ephesians 4:29

17. What can you learn from these passages?

Ephesians 4:30
CCC 698
CCC 1274
CCC 1296

18. What must you put away? Ephesians 4:31

19. How must Christians relate to others? Ephesians 4:32

20. How and why must we forgive others? Ephesians 4:32, CCC 2842

* Is there someone you need to ask God to help you to forgive?

CHAPTER 21

Marriage in Christ
Ephesians 5

This is a great mystery, and I mean in reference to Christ and the Church;
however, let each one of you love his wife as himself,
and let the wife see that she respects her husband.
Ephesians 5:32–33

Imitate God and walk in love. In the Garden of Eden, God established marriage as the first human institution, before criminal justice, government, education, priesthood, or anything else. Marriage remains the bedrock of human society. When marriages are strong and healthy, the society flourishes. When marriages fail, government and others must take up the slack to provide for abandoned women and children. A stable marriage provides the best environment for children to grow and prosper. Studies also show that married men enjoy better health and longevity than single, widowed, or divorced men. God said, *"It is not good that the man should be alone"* (Genesis 2:18), but there are plenty of lonely people around.

The sexual revolution of the late 1960s impacted society profoundly. Ignoring God, people decided to have sex, whenever and with whomever they pleased, as long as precautions were taken to avoid pregnancy. The advent of the birth control pill promised that marriages would be stronger, as women could have sex at any time without a concern for pregnancy. Pope (Saint) Paul VI gave a prophetic warning in *Humanae Vitae* that was largely mocked and ignored. What resulted? Sexually transmitted diseases became epidemic. Abortions and divorces are common. Broken hearts and relationships litter the horizon. What went wrong?

God is love. He invented love and marriage and knows how it can best work. Saint Paul tells us to imitate God and walk in love, as Christ loved us. Christ loved us with a *sacrificial love*. Jesus gave Himself up as a sacrificial offering, which recalls the fragrant offerings of the Old Testament sacrifices. Jesus put our need for salvation over and above His own needs. Jesus put *us* first!

Shun immorality. *But immorality and all impurity or covetousness must not even be named among you, as is fitting among saints* (Ephesians 5:3). Filthy talk and levity permeates television, radio, books, and entertainment. Christians must be countercultural. Fools forfeit their inheritance in the kingdom of God by choosing immorality, impurity, and disobedience to God. Before conversion to Christ, many walked in sin and darkness. But, once the light of Christ is revealed, God gives believers the grace to walk in the light. Christians must strive to do what is good, right, and true. Christians leave behind pagan ways and strive to do what is just and pleasing to the Lord. Believers must not get drunk with wine, but rather be filled with the Holy Spirit in order to give glory and praise to God.

Confusion abounds on the nature and definition of marriage. Is marriage simply a deep friendship or romantic attachment of any two individuals who profess to be "in love?" Is this a 50/50 proposition for as long as love lasts or until someone better comes along? What did God intend in Genesis, and what is Paul expounding about in these passages? What, in essence, is marriage?

Marriage—Professor Robert P. George, American legal and political philosopher at Princeton, defines marriage as **"a conjugal relationship based on sexual complementarity, naturally ordered to the procreation of children, which is permanent and exclusive."** Marriage is a comprehensive, all-encompassing union of a man and a woman for life. Professor George posits that when a baby is born anywhere, you will find a woman—the mother. The question is, "Where will the father be? Will you find a man anywhere in the vicinity of this mother and child?"

Marriage comes into existence when a man and a woman, forswearing all others, through an "act of irrevocable personal consent" freely give themselves to one another. At the heart of the act establishing marriage is a free, self-determining choice on the part of the man and the woman, through which they give themselves a new and lasting identity. . . . Prior to this act of irrevocable personal consent, the man and the woman are separate individuals, replaceable and substitutable in each other's lives. But, in and through this act, they make each other unique and irreplaceable. . . . [They] pledge to one another that they will honor and foster the "goods" or "blessings" of marriage, namely, the procreation and education of children and steadfast faithful love.

The reality of these "goods" is beautifully revealed in the marital or conjugal act . . . that manifests uniquely and fittingly the sexual complementarity of husband and wife as male and female. . . . Males and females express their sexuality—their giving and receiving—in complementary ways: the male gives in a receiving sort of way, while the female receives in a giving sort of way . . .

Non-married men and women are capable of engaging in genital acts because they are endowed with genitals. But when non-married men and women have sex, they do not, and *cannot, give* themselves to each other and *receive* each other. . . . They have refused to make each other irreplaceable and non-substitutable persons; they have refused to make each other *spouses*.
William E. May, *Marriage: The Rock on Which the Family is Built*,
(San Francisco: Ignatius Press, 1995) 20, 26–27

God created humans. God brought Eve to Adam as a helpmate and spouse. God has the right to define what marriage is and to reveal how marriage will best work. Saint Paul recalls the Genesis passages, and then he further reveals that Christian marriage should become an icon of God's love. As Christ loves His body—the Church—and gave His life for her, so husbands should love their wives. Wives have the right to receive love and care, to be subordinate to love. And husbands have the responsibility to love, cherish, protect, and provide for their wives. Husbands deserve love and respect in return. O. Henry's short story, *The Gift of the Magi,* describes a poor, newlywed couple who have no Christmas gifts to give one another. The wife sells her beautiful long hair to buy her husband a watch chain. The husband sells his watch to buy his wife combs for her hair. They each give up their best, out of love for the other. Jesus gave up everything to save us!

Ephesians 5:22 may be most contentious verse in the Bible. It is bracketed now, and optional, in Mass readings. *Be subject to one another out of reverence for Christ. Wives, be submissive to your husbands, as to the Lord* (Ephesians 5:21–22). While politically incorrect and offensive to modern sensibilities, Pope (Saint) John Paul II gives inspiration and clarity to these verses in his teachings on *The Theology of the Body,* which remain a profound gift to the Church, worth studying.

The mutual relation of husband and wife should flow from their common relationship with Christ. . . . The author speaks of the mutual subjection of the spouses, husband and wife, and in this way he explains the words he will write afterward on the subjection of the wife to the husband. . . . In saying this, the author does not intend to say that the husband is the lord of the wife and the interpersonal pact proper to marriage is a pact of domination of the husband over the wife. Instead, he expresses a different concept—that the wife can and should find in her relationship with Christ, who is the one Lord of both the spouses, the motivation of that relationship with her husband which flows from the very essence of marriage and of the family. . . . The husband and the wife are in fact "subject to one another," and are mutually subordinated to one another. The source of this mutual subjection is to be found in Christian pietas, and its expression is love.

The author of the letter underlines this love in a special way, addressing himself to husbands. He writes: "Husbands, love your wives . . ." By expressing himself in this way, he removes any fear that might have arisen (given the modern sensitivity) from the previous phrase: "Wives be subject to your husbands." Love excludes every kind of subjection whereby the wife becomes a servant or a slave of the husband, an object of unilateral domination. Love makes the husband simultaneously subject to the wife, and thereby subject to the Lord himself, just as the wife to the husband. The community, or unity which they should establish through marriage, is constituted by a reciprocal donation of self, which is also a mutual subjection. Christ is the source and at the same time the model of that subjection.

Pope (Saint) John Paul II, *The Theology of the Body,*
Boston, MA: Pauline Books, 1997, 310

Paul invites Christians to envision and practice a deeper understanding of Christian marriage than has ever been presented before in the history of the world. Ancient household codes only addressed men, never women. Jesus had washed the feet of His disciples and gave an example of humble service. Jesus listened to, healed, and fed people when He was exhausted and hungry. He suffered a painful, humiliating death on the cross to redeem humanity. In looking at the cross, believers can find the grace and strength to give humble service, deference, and submission to the needs and directives of another. Only by abiding in Jesus can married persons fulfill His command to love one another (John 15:12). Contemporary culture insists: "Take care of Number One. It's my body. I did it MY way. You deserve a break today. Me first! Me first!" The Christian says, "You go first. Let me serve you."

Christian marriage invites each spouse to make a total and complete gift of self to the other. Marriage requires self-donation that is exclusive and unreserved. Each makes a total gift of self to the other. Jesus gave everything. He withheld nothing. Jesus did not offer a 50/50 proposition to sinful humanity. He paid the full price.

Father John Riccardo provides further insight into these verses. "Paul is expecting the husband, as one reborn in Christ through baptism, to participate in the life of Christ, to make his own the actions and attitudes of the Lord. There is quite simply no way that anyone can argue that these actions and attitudes are oppressive, domineering, offensive, or not in keeping with the dignity of the other person involved. Ephesians 5:23 holds out to the husband a model of headship which is to be expressed by his taking the lead, the initiative, in being a servant to his wife, just as Christ took the lead and poured out his life in service. His life, including his willingness to lay down his very life for her, is to be a making present of the life and love of Christ for her. His wife has a claim upon his whole attention."
Father John Riccardo, STL, *Mutual Submission, [dissertation]*
Pope John Paul II Institute for Studies on Marriage and the Family, 36–37

Engaged couples focus on romantic love. Wedding details—guests, flowers, photographers, clothes, music, honeymoon plans—occupy their attention prior to the wedding. Faith, communication, self-donation, finances, openness to life, child-rearing practices, and in-laws usually receive less attention. While romantic love blesses every married couple, mutual respect, self-denial, and sacrificial love are essential in building a stable, lifelong, faithful marital relationship.

Marriage is the best anti-poverty program ever invented. Society works best when marriages are strong, loving, and stable. The Catholic Church values marriage. Engaged Encounters and Pre-Cana programs strive to prepare couples for marriage. Premarital testing and counseling help couples identify red flags, which may become serious problems in the marriage. Marriage Encounters help couples to keep the flame burning during the hectic, busy years. Retrouvaille provides help for wounded marriages. Ideally, married couples should stay together. But Paul recognizes that sometimes separation becomes necessary (1 Corinthians 7:10–11). Alcoholism, drug abuse, gambling, pornography, adultery, or violence may make it necessary for a spouse to separate for safety. The Church holds up the ideal for a strong sacramental marriage. Catholics refrain from judging the innocent victims who suffer the pain of broken vows and shattered marriages. It takes two to make a strong, healthy marriage. But it only takes one to destroy that marriage.

In almost every Catholic wedding, you will hear about God's creation of Eve and Adam's response. *"This at last is bone of my bones and flesh of my flesh. . . . Therefore a man leaves his father and his mother and clings to his wife and they become one flesh"* (Genesis 2:23–24). A mature man and woman choose to leave their families of origin and cleave to one another to create a new family. You have also heard Paul's exhortation to love. *Love is patient and kind; love is not jealous or boastful; it is not arrogant or rude. Love does not insist on its own way. . . . Love bears all things, believes all things, hopes all things, endures all things* (1 Corinthians 13:4–7). These verses ring poetic in the church. Living them out faithfully, day to day, in good times and in hard times, requires all the grace of the sacrament of matrimony and often heroic virtue as well.

The witness of marriages of loving newlyweds and also faithful, elderly couples, married for decades, still devoted and serving one another in the twilight of life, illustrates the beauty of God's original plan, as it unfolds. See and emulate the dignity of the human persons, reflecting the image of God's love in the Trinity, mirrored in God's creation of marital love, lived out in the sacrament of matrimony.

Lily and Robert Tobar met while students at the University of Miami. Robert completed medical school and became a cardiologist. Lily completed a PhD in clinical psychology and began her counseling career. They married in 1993 at Saint Patrick Catholic Church in Miami Beach and were blessed with three children.

A feminist at the time, Lily held very firm views on how men and women should accept totally equal roles and share equivalent responsibilities in everything. She experienced the first ten years of her marriage as somewhat difficult and challenging. With both parents working full time and raising their three active children, arguments and power struggles crept into their marriage.

Lily and Robert's marriage changed dramatically when Lily attended a Bible study that invited her to reflect on Ephesians 5:22–30. The Lord softened her heart. Lily realized that she was not putting Robert first and was not submitting to him in the way that God was asking her to do. As an experiment, Lily tried to put Robert first and to defer to him, and she was shocked at how dramatically Robert changed! Immediately, Robert became more loving, protective, and giving to her! He began to give her everything she had ever wanted, and greater peace and intimacy blossomed in their marriage. Robert and Lily are now part of the marriage and family life ministry at Saint Helen Church in Vero Beach, Florida. They give talks and mentor engaged couples in their parish. God's perfect plan works!

Reflections on Women

William Golding, the author of *The Lord of the Flies,* suggested in a May 2010 interview that women are not inferior to men and are foolish to consider themselves equals, because in many ways women may be superior to men.

"Whatever you give a woman, she will make greater. If you give her sperm, she'll give you a baby. If you give her a house, she'll give you a home. If you give her groceries, she'll give you a meal. If you give her a smile, she'll give you her heart. She multiplies and enlarges what is given to her."

"My quest to understand Our Lady started even before I was married with children. It came to my attention that most of the things promoted by women in our culture—being outspoken, assertive, independent, and ambitious—weren't producing the kind of happiness I expected. I started paying attention to music, poetry, and movies, anywhere I could find evidence of what made for truly timeless and great women, not just those propped up by our culture.

And what did I find? Remarkable and beautiful portrayals of women using interior capacities I had never thought about before: kindness, compassion, listening, anticipating the needs of others, sincerity, and goodness. Getting married and having children only made me go deeper to find and live these newly discovered virtues. I marveled at the fruits—my friends got closer; my children grew contented; my husband became more loving—all because I turned from self-absorption to looking to the needs of others. Living these virtues was the missing piece of the puzzle I couldn't see. I needed to live Mary's virtues to understand her from the inside. We see them in Scripture: silence, obedience, kindness, meekness, and tenderness. I couldn't find comfort in Our Lady before this realization because her virtues were foreign to me."

Carrie Gress, *The Anti-Mary Exposed,*
(Charlotte, NC: TAN Books, 2019), 167–168

1. How can a believer become Christ-like?

Ephesians 5:1
CCC 1694

2. Compare the following passages.

Exodus 29:18
Ezekiel 20:41
Ephesians 5:2
CCC 616

3. Summarize Ephesians 5:3–14 in your own words.

4. What can you learn from these passages?

Ephesians 5:15–20
CCC 672
CCC 2826

* What helps you to discern the will of God for you?

5. What is a Christian called to be, after baptism?

Ephesians 5:21
CCC 1269

6. What can you learn from these passages?

Ephesians 5:22
Ephesians 5:23
Ephesians 5:24

7. What can you learn about sacramental marriage?

Genesis 2:23–25
CCC 1601
CCC 1603
CCC 1604
CCC 1605

* Identify a Catholic marriage that reflects Christ's love for His Church.

8. What can you learn about the family?

CCC 2202
CCC 2203
CCC 2204
CCC 2205
CCC 2206

9. What must husbands do in a Christian marriage?

Ephesians 5:25
Ephesians 5:28
CCC 1641
CCC 1642

10. Who helps married persons in a sacramental marriage? CCC 1624

11. What was Christ's goal in loving His bride? Ephesians 5:26–27

12. Explore the mystery and the challenge presented in Ephesians 5.

CCC 772
CCC 773
CCC 796
CCC 1426

13. Find the fulfillment of the spotless bride.

Ephesians 5:27
Revelation 21:1–2
CCC 756–757

14. How does a man care for his own flesh? Ephesians 5:29

15. Give a practical example of Ephesians 5:28b.

* Describe an example of a Christ-like husband and father.

* Describe an example of a Christ-like wife and mother.

16. Use a dictionary and the Catechism to define "marriage." CCC 1601

17. What three verbs describe marriage from Ephesians 5:31?

18. What must husbands do in Ephesians 5:33a?

19. What must wives do in Ephesians 5:33b?

20. List practical ways in which husbands and wives can show love and respect.

Husbands	Wives

CHAPTER 22

The Armor of God
Ephesians 6

Finally, be strong in the Lord and in the strength of his might.
Put on the whole armor of God,
that you may be able to stand against the wiles of the devil.
Ephesians 6:10–11

Parents and children—After addressing husbands and wives on the importance of healthy marital relationships, Paul turns his focus to family relationships between parents and children. *Children, obey your parents in the Lord, for this is right. "Honor your father and mother" (this is the first commandment with a promise), "that it may be well with you and that you may live long on the earth"* (Ephesians 6:1–3). Here, Paul recalls God's promise given to Moses on Mount Sinai, for the Chosen People, and recorded with the Ten Commandments in Exodus 20:12. Enjoying God's promises flows from obedience to God's Word.

Obedient, well-mannered children delight their parents and other adults. Moreover, adult children continue to show honor and respect to their parents. *For a man's glory comes from honoring his father, and it is a disgrace for children not to respect their mother. O son, help your father in his old age, and do not grieve him as long as he lives* (Sirach 3:11–12). One of the stressors in marriage can occur when a married couple becomes sandwiched between providing for the needs of their children, while at the same time caring for aging parents. Furthermore, in earlier times, extended families clustered close to one another. But now adult children may live far away from their elderly parents.

Jesus models obedience to Mary and Joseph when He ends the discussion with the teachers in the temple and obediently returns home to Nazareth with His parents. *And he went down with them and came to Nazareth, and was obedient to them. . . . And Jesus increased in wisdom and in stature, and in favor with God and man* (Luke 2:51–52). God prizes the virtue of obedience. Saul learned this lesson the hard way from the prophet Samuel. *"Behold, to obey is better than sacrifice, and to listen than the fat of rams. For rebellion is as the sin of divination, and stubbornness is as iniquity and idolatry. Because you have rejected the word of the LORD, he has also rejected you from being king"* (1 Samuel 15:22–23).

Fathers, do not provoke your children to anger, but bring them up in the discipline and instruction of the Lord (Ephesians 6:4). Through the grace of the sacrament of matrimony, parents have the privilege and responsibility of *evangelizing their children* (CCC 2225). The Second Vatican Council yielded pride of place to parents for the privilege and responsibility of the education and faith formation of their children. Parents evangelize their children by their words and by their example.

Christian spouses, in virtue of the sacrament of Matrimony, whereby they signify and partake of the mystery of that unity and fruitful love which exists between Christ and His Church, help each other to attain to holiness in their married life and in the rearing and education of their children. By reason of their state and rank in life they have their own special gift among the people of God. From the wedlock of Christians there comes the family, in which new citizens of human society are born, who by the grace of the Holy Spirit received in baptism are made children of God, thus perpetuating the people of God through the centuries. **The family is, so to speak, the domestic church. In it parents should, by their word and example, be the first preachers of the faith to their children;** they should encourage them in the vocation, which is proper to each of them, fostering with special care vocation to a sacred state.   *Lumen Gentium,* November 21, 1964, 11.2

In the past, some Catholic parents routinely relegated the privilege and responsibility for the faith formation of their children to the priests and religious. However, parents have the primary responsibility before God to introduce their children to God and to bring up their children in the faith. Prayer in the home, sacraments, and worship at Sunday Mass together as a family provide a faith foundation for children to fall back upon when they encounter challenging times.

Parents invest energy seeking out the best schools, finest athletic programs, and music and enrichment opportunities for their children. Sometimes parents try to live vicariously through their children, lavishing them with privileges they lacked or burdening them with unrealistic expectations. Parents walk a narrow road between laxity on one side and harsh severity on the other. Children need love, discipline, and boundaries in order to develop their unique potential as God's children.

Slavery is in the Bible! During the first century, many people were enslaved. About one-third of the population at that time were slaves. Sometimes slaves were able to earn or buy their freedom. While Paul is not advocating slavery, he speaks to the condition existing at the time. *Slaves, be obedient to those who are your earthly masters, with fear and trembling, in singleness of heart, as to Christ . . . knowing that whatever good any one does, he will receive the same again from the Lord, whether he is a slave or free* (Ephesians 6:5, 8).

Unfortunately, in many countries, including England and the United States, slave owners and slave merchants misused Sacred Scripture in an attempt to justify an evil and inhumane practice. This reveals an abuse and distortion of biblical texts. One must not manipulate Scriptures to advance a wicked cause. The British Christian William Wilberforce spent his whole adult life lobbying for the end of the legal slave trade in England. After leaving the Royal British Navy, John Newton (1725–1807) became involved in the Atlantic slave trade. After a horrific storm at sea, John Newton repented of his ways, converted to Christianity, and left the slave trade. He later wrote the beautiful, familiar hymn "Amazing Grace."

> The seventh commandment forbids acts or enterprises that for any reason—selfish or ideological, commercial, or totalitarian—lead to the *enslavement of human beings,* to their being bought, sold and exchanged like merchandise, in disregard for their personal dignity. It is a sin against the dignity of persons and their fundamental rights to reduce them by violence to their productive value or to a source of profit. St. Paul directed a Christian master to treat his Christian slave "no longer as a slave but more than a slave, as a beloved brother . . . both in the flesh and in the Lord" (Philemon 16). CCC 2414

Sadly, slavery continues to exist in our world. Today, human traffickers transport girls, women, and young boys to foreign countries for the purpose of prostitution. Even good parents can be deceived and sell their children to merchants, believing that the child will be taken to a rich country for honest work or a proper marriage. The Catholic Church forbids this practice and endeavors to minister to vulnerable people who have become victims of exploitation or sex slavery.

Christians, stand strong in the Lord. Paul's final admonition exhorts believers to stand strong in the Lord and to rely on the strength of His might. Christians wage a constant spiritual battle against the forces of evil. Jesus was tempted by the devil in the wilderness, at the very beginning of His ministry (Matthew 4:1–11). Jesus defeated Satan, sin, and death on the cross. But, while the final victory has been accomplished, the devil continues to roam about the world tempting believers until Jesus comes again in glory. Saint Irenaeus recaps God's plan of salvation.

> For the Church . . . has received from the Apostles . . . the faith in one God, Father Almighty, the Creator of heaven and earth . . . and in one Jesus Christ, the Son of God, who became flesh for our salvation; and in the Holy Spirit, who announced through the prophets . . . the birth from a Virgin, and the passion, and the resurrection from the dead, and the bodily ascension into heaven of the beloved Christ Jesus our Lord, and His coming from heaven in the glory of the Father to re-establish all things; and the raising up again of all flesh of all humanity, in order that to Jesus Christ our Lord and God and Savior and King, in accord with the approval of the invisible Father, every knee shall bend of those in heaven and on earth and under the earth, and that every tongue shall confess Him, and that He may make just judgment of them all; and that He may send the spiritual forces of wickedness, and the angels who transgressed and became apostates, and the impious, unjust, lawless and blasphemous among men, into everlasting fire; and that He may grant life, immortality, and surround with eternal glory the just and the holy, and those who have kept His commands and who have persevered in His love, either from their beginning or from their repentance.
>
> Saint Irenaeus (AD 140–202), *Against Heresies,* 1, 10, 1

Finally, be strong in the Lord and in the strength of his might. Put on the whole armor of God, that you may be able to stand against the wiles of the devil. For we are not contending against flesh and blood, but against the principalities, against the powers, against the world rulers of this present darkness, against the spiritual hosts of wickedness in the heavenly places (Ephesians 6:10–12). People are not the enemy. Demons and evil spirits wage war against the followers of Jesus. Wicked people do evil things because Satan seduces them. The enemy is demonic, not human. Christians pray for fallen sinners and wage spiritual combat against evil. The best means for fighting evil are prayer and fasting.

Defend yourself from the enemy with the whole armor of God:

> ➤ Wrap around your waist—the belt of truth.
>> *I am the way, and the truth, and the life* (John 14:6).
>> *Speak the truth in love* (Ephesians 4:15).

> ➤ Protect your heart with—the breastplate of righteousness.
>> *Unless your righteousness exceeds that of the scribes and Pharisees,*
>>> *you will never enter the kingdom of heaven* (Matthew 5:20).

> ➤ Shod your feet with—the gospel of peace.
>> *"Peace I leave with you; my peace I give to you"* (John 14:27).

> ➤ Lift the shield of faith—to avoid the flaming darts of the Evil One.
>> *And Jesus answered them, "Have faith in God"* (Mark 11:22).

> ➤ Cover your head with—the helmet of salvation.
>> *In him you also, who have heard the word of truth,*
>>> *the gospel of your salvation, and have believed in him,*
>>> *were sealed with the promised Holy Spirit* (Ephesians 1:13).

> ➤ Wield the Sword of the Spirit—the Word of God.
>> *The grass withers, and the flower fails,*
>>> *but the word of the Lord abides forever* (1 Peter 1:24–25).

Pray constantly. *Pray at all times in the Spirit, with all prayer and supplication. To that end keep alert with all perseverance, making supplication for all the saints, and also for me, that utterance may be given me in opening my mouth boldly to proclaim the mystery of the gospel* (Ephesians 6:18–19). Paul makes repeated exhortations in his letters for believers to pray constantly. *Rejoice always, pray constantly, give thanks in all circumstances; for this is the will of God in Christ Jesus for you* (1 Thessalonians 5:16–17).

Paul's letters to the Romans and Ephesians provide doctrinal truths concerning salvation by faith in Jesus Christ and practical instruction for living the Christian life. Centuries after these words were penned, they continue to bring truth, hope, and direction to believers. Christians today can find peace, love, and joy in studying these letters and applying these truths to everyday life.

Saint Josephine Bakhita
Former Slave and Patron Saint of Sudan

Josephine Bakhita was born into a prominent family in the Darfur region of the Sudan around 1869. Her father, a well-respected, and prosperous man, belonged to the prestigious Daju people; his brother was the tribal chief. She enjoyed a loving family with three brothers and three sisters and lived a happy, carefree life, without knowing suffering in her early years. Sadly, that would all change.

Arab slave traders kidnapped her at age seven, then forced her to walk barefoot for six hundred miles. She was sold and resold a dozen times in the markets. Having forgotten the name her parents had given her, the kidnappers assigned her the name Bakhita, which means "fortunate." Suffering severe brutality and torture during her bondage, she was cut with a knife one-hundred-fourteen times. Salt was poured into her wounds, causing permanent scars. She was forced to convert to Islam.

In the Sudanese capital, Bakhita was sold to an Italian consul and later arrived in Italy, where she was entrusted to the care of the Canossian Sisters of the Institute of Catechumens in Venice. It was there that Bakhita came to know about the Christian God. "Seeing the sun, the moon and the stars, I said to myself: 'Who could be the Master of these beautiful things?' And I felt a great desire to see him, to know him and to pay him homage," said Bakhita.

Cardinal Giuseppe Sarto, who later became Pope Pius X, met Bakhita (now Josephine Margaret), and on January 9, 1890, administered her sacraments of initiation—Baptism, Holy Communion, and Confirmation. Sister Josephine Margaret and Fortunata entered the convent and professed her final vows as a Daughter of Charity in 1896. Later, she was assigned to the convent at Schio, in the Italian province of Vicenza, where she spent the rest of her life.

During World War II, the villagers of Schio regarded Sister Josephine as their protector. Although bombs fell on the village, not one person died. During her forty-two years in Schio, she worked as a cook, sacristan, and doorkeeper. She was in frequent contact with the people in the local community. Her gentleness, calming voice, and ever-present smile became well known, and Vicenzans still refer to her as Sor Moretta, "Little Brown Sister," or Madre Moretta, "Black Mother." Her fellow religious sisters noticed her special charisma and reputation for sanctity. Sister Josephine Bakhita's story, Storia Meravigliosa, by Ida Zanolini, published in 1931, made her famous throughout Italy.

Sister Josephine died on February 8, 1947. Thousands of people came to pay their respects. Pope (Saint) John Paul II canonized Saint Josephine Bakhita on October 1, 2000. She is venerated as a modern African saint, and her life story illuminates the brutal practice of slavery. She has been adopted as the patron saint of Sudan.

1. What can you learn from these passages?

Exodus 20:12
Ephesians 6:1–3

2. How does the Catechism explain this command?

CCC 2197
CCC 2198
CCC 2200
CCC 2215
CCC 2216

3. What can you learn about fatherhood?

Proverbs 3:11–12
Sirach 3:9a
Ephesians 6:4
CCC 2214

* Describe a really obedient child or children you know.

4. Who is responsible for the education and formation of children?

Ephesians 6:4b
CCC 2223
CCC 2225
CCC 2226

5. What advice does Paul give to slaves? Ephesians 6:5–8

6. What advice is given to Masters? Ephesians 6:9

7. How does the Catholic Church see slavery? CCC 2414

8. Who will deal with Masters who are harsh and threatening? Ephesians 6:9

9. What does Paul encourage in Ephesians 6:10–11, and why?

10. Who is the enemy? Ephesians 6:12

11. Explain the armor of God. Ephesians 6:13–17

belt
breastplate
shoes
shield
helmet
sword

12. Compare these passages.

Isaiah 11:5
Isaiah 59:17
Ephesians 6:14–17

13. What must all Christians do faithfully?

Matthew 26:41
Ephesians 6:18
1 Thessalonians 5:8

* How and when do you pray daily?

14. What else must a believer do?

Ephesians 6:18b
Hebrews 12:1
CCC 2728

15. Use a dictionary or the Catechism to define "perseverance." CCC 162

16. For whom else should Christians pray? Ephesians 6:18–19

17. What specific prayer request does Paul make? Ephesians 6:19

18. How does Paul describe himself? Ephesians 6:20

19. What is Paul's goal in sending this letter? Ephesians 6:22b

20. With what blessing does Paul close his epistle? Ephesians 6:23–24

* What was your most challenging verse in this Bible Study?

** What was your favorite verse in this Bible Study?

*** Did anything become clearer to you in studying Romans and Ephesians?

**** Express your gratitude by offering to pray for a member of your group.

COME AND SEE

Catholic Bible Study

About Our Authors

Bishop Jan Liesen, SSD – of the Netherlands was on the Papal Theological Commission. He wrote *Wisdom* and *The Gospel of Mark* and teaches on the videos.

Bishop Liesen, Dr. Manhardt, Archbishop Byrnes

Laurie Watson Manhardt, PhD – the University of Michigan, wrote several chapters of commentary in each book and all of the home study questions.

Archbishop Michael J. Byrnes, STD – of Guam, studied Scripture at the Pontifical Gregorian University in Rome and taught at Sacred Heart Major Seminary in Detroit. He collaborated on Romans and appears on the videos.

Father Ponessa

Father Joseph Ponessa, SSD – studied Sacred Scripture at the Biblicum, and is the primary author of *The Gospels of Matthew, Luke,* and *John, Genesis, Moses and the Torah, David and the Psalms, Prophets and Apostles, Acts and Letters,* and many other books.

Monsignor Charles Kosanke, STD – studied at the Pontifical Gregorian University in Rome, taught at Sacred Heart Major Seminary, and was the rector of Saints Cyril and Methodius Seminary in Orchard Lake, Michigan. He is the primary author of *Isaiah.*

Sharon Doran, MA – studied Scripture at the Augustine Institute in Denver, and founded the Seeking Truth Bible Study in Omaha. Sharon wrote *Judges, Amos and Hosea* and appears on many videos. Sharon and her husband Steve are the parents of five sons.

Sharon Doran

Monsignor Jan Majernik, STD – a native of Slovakia, earned a doctorate in Sacred Scripture from the Franciscan School of Biblical Studies in Jerusalem. He studied biblical archeology and biblical languages at the Hebrew University in Israel. He is the primary author of *The Synoptics.*

Father Andreas Hoeck, SSD – was born in Cologne, Germany and earned his doctorate at the Pontifical Biblical Institute in Rome, where he wrote his dissertation on the book of Revelation. He is the author of *Ezekiel, Hebrews, Revelation,* and is the academic dean of the seminary in Denver.

Basic, Foundational Books

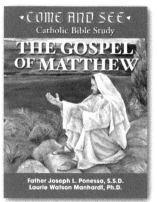

The Gospel of Matthew — The first book of the New Testament looks at the life and teachings of Jesus Christ in this 22 week Bible study.

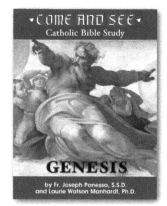

Genesis — Look at creatio through the lens of scienc and the lives of Adam and Ev Noah, Abraham, Isaac an Jacob, in this 22 chapter stud

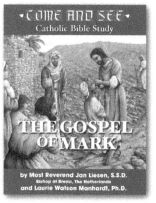

The Gospel of Mark— Study the first gospel written, recounting the life and ministry of Jesus in this 18 week study.

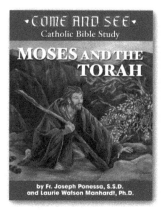

Moses and the Torah – Study *Exodus, Leviticu Numbers*, and *Deuteronom* in this 22 chapter boo completing the Pentateuch.

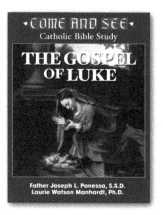

The Gospel of Luke — This 21 week study begins with the infancy narratives and early life of Jesus and continues to the Ascension of Our Lord.

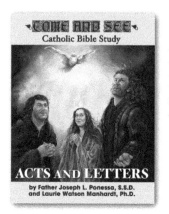

Acts and Letters — Explor the early Church throug Luke's *Acts of the Apostl* and Paul's letters in this 2 week Bible study.

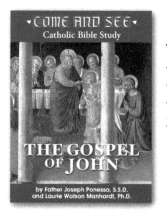

The Gospel of John — Study the life of Jesus from John's theological perspective, and see the sacraments emerge in this 21 week study.

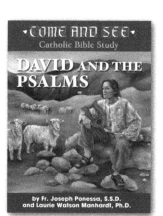

David and the Psalms – This 22 week study examine Ruth, Samuel and David, an their lives and prayers in *Ruth 1 and 2 Samuel, Psalms*.

Advanced, Challenging Books

Wisdom — Bishop Liesen writes commentary on the Wisdom literature, the poetry of the Bible – *Job, Proverbs Song of Solomon, Wisdom, and Sirach*.

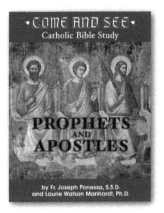

Prophets and Apostles — Old Testament prophets looked forward to God's promised Messiah while the New Testament apostles find fulfillment of prophecy in the life of Jesus.

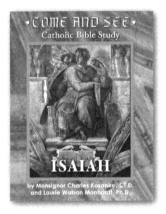

Isaiah — Called the fifth Gospel, this Old Testament prophet points to Jesus of Nazareth, the Suffering Servant and Redeemer of the world, in this 22 week study.

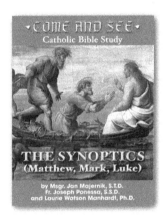

The Synoptics — Compare *Matthew, Mark,* and *Luke's* accounts of the life of Jesus as you journey through the Holy Land in this 22 week overview of the Gospels.

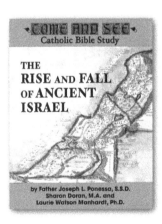

The Rise and Fall of Ancient Israel — Study the history of ancient Israel in this 21 week study of *Joshua, Judges, 1 and 2 Kings, 1 and 2 Chronicles, Amos, Hosea,* and *Jeremiah.*

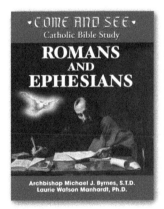

Romans and Ephesians — This 22 week study covers two beloved Pauline prison epistles: Romans and Ephesians, to provide deep and profound theological insights.

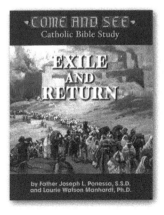

Exile and Return — *Tobit, Judith, Esther, Ezra, Nehemiah, 1 and 2 Maccabees* show how God worked in the lives of the Jewish people as they return to the Holy Land from the Babylonian exile.

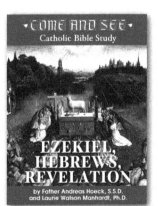

Ezekiel, Hebrews, Revelation — The Prophet Ezekiel has amazing visions similar to those of John revealed in the book of *Revelation. The Letter to the Hebrews* reveals Jesus the High Priest in this 22 week study.

Spanish Bible Studies

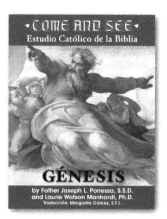

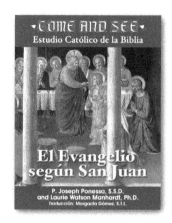

~ Endorsements ~

"The *Come and See ~ Catholic Bible Study* series provides an in depth and detailed analysis of the books of the Bible and is both an educational and spiritual way of approaching the word of God as revealed in Sacred Scripture."

Most Reverend Gerald M. Barbarito,
Bishop of Palm Beach, FL

"We found this Bible Study to be unique in several ways. It required personal preparation, reading the chapter and its excellent commentary provided by the authors, and answering questions that connected the chapter with other passages in the Old and New Testament and in the *Catechism of the Catholic Church*. The questions also invited us to personal reflection and to apply the teachings to our personal lives and to the problems of today. Thus, we learned a lot!"

Dr. and Mrs. Renato Gadenz, Eatontown, NJ

"The *Come and See ~ Catholic Bible Studies* are excellent and are helping men and women all over the country better understand the Bible and its relationship to the Catholic Church… Highly recommended."

Ralph Martin, S.T.D.,
President, Renewal Ministries, Ann Arbor
Director, New Evangelization,
Sacred Heart Seminary, Detroit, MI

"Certainly this is THE BEST study on the market. Not just because it is the least expensive, no, but, because it is so well done. I've researched extensively. It IS the best. Our parish is in the 10th year of *Come and See ~ Catholic Bible Study* and loving it!"

Chris Snyder,
Marlborough, MA

Come and See KIDS Books

Come and See KIDS is a Bible Study series written for pre-school to early elementary school age children. These companion books to the adult series could also be used alone.

- Bible memory verses and a Bible story
- Coloring pages illustrating the Bible story
- Craft activities for the child to make with a little bit of help

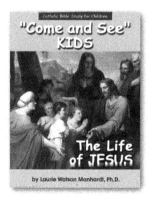

Emmaus Road Publishing
www.EmmausRoad.org
(740) 264-9535

Come and See ~ Catholic Bible Study
www.CatholicBibleStudy.net
(772) 321-4034

Prayer Requests

My Small Group

CPSIA information can be obtained
at www.ICGtesting.com
Printed in the USA
LVHW010808080421
683690LV00006B/39